DIPLOMA DECEPTION

How the TEA4CH™ Method Transforms Teaching and Elevates Education

MICHELLE VAN DE SANDE

Copyright © 2025
MICHELLE VAN DE SANDE
DIPLOMA DECEPTION
*How the TEA4CH™ Method Transforms Teaching
and Elevates Education*
All rights reserved.

No part of this publication may be reproduced, distributed, or transmitted in any form or by any means, including photocopying, recording, or other electronic or mechanical methods, without the prior written permission of the author, except in the case of brief quotations embodied in critical reviews and certain other non-commercial uses permitted by copyright law.

MICHELLE VAN DE SANDE
For permission requests, contact the publisher at:
Named by Design, Rapid City, South Dakota
www.TEA4CH.com

Printed Worldwide
First Printing 2025
First Edition 2025

10 9 8 7 6 5 4 3 2 1

ISBN (Paperback): 978-0-9862712-5-0
ISBN (eBook): 978-0-9862712-5-0

Interior Book Design by Walt's Book Design
www.waltsbookdesign.com

Edited by Marni MacRae

Disclaimer: This book is a work of nonfiction. Every effort has been made to provide accurate and up-to-date information based on research, professional experience, and available data. The views expressed are those of the author. The publisher and author disclaim any liability for any loss or damages resulting from the use of information contained in this book.
Names and identifying details of individuals (other than public figures) have been changed when necessary to protect privacy.

DIPLOMA DECEPTION

Dedication

To my husband, Peter, who believed in me and in all God created me to do, even when no one else did. Your faith and unwavering support made this possible.

To every student I have had the privilege of teaching, you opened my eyes to what education could and should be. You showed me what was broken, and you inspired me to fight for something better so that none of you would be lost or forgotten.

To the students who never stopped trying, to the teachers who never stopped believing, and to the parents who entrusted their children's futures to education.

This book is for you.

Epigraph

"Over 41% of recent college graduates are underemployed, and two-thirds of employers say new hires are not fully prepared."

— Federal Reserve Bank of New York, 2025; Deloitte, 2025

"The function of education is to teach one to think intensively and to think critically.
Intelligence plus character—that is the goal of true education."

— Martin Luther King, Jr.

"You will know the truth, and the truth will set you free."

— John 8:32

Table of Contents

Preface 1

Introduction 5

Part I 13

  The Deception

  Chapter One 15

    The Illusion of Success

  Chapter Two 25

    The Shocking Truth About Teaching

  Chapter Three 35

    Why Lecture Fails

  Chapter Four 43

    What Students Really Need

  Chapter Five 55

    Real-World vs. Classroom

  Chapter Six 63

    The Missing Feedback Loop

  Chapter Seven 73

    Learning That Lasts

Part II 81

  The Transformation

  Chapter Eight 83

    From Deception to Transformation

  Chapter Nine 91

    The Cost of Doing Nothing

Chapter Ten 97
    Parents as Partners
Chapter Eleven 107
    The Digital Classroom Dilemma
Chapter Twelve 117
    The Future of Education
Closing Vision 123
Epilogue 125
References 131
Call to Action 135
Final Word 137
About the Author 139

Preface

For more than three decades, I have watched education shift before my eyes. At first, I thought the changes were temporary... new programs, new initiatives, new theories that would come and go like passing trends. But as the years went by, I realized the shifts weren't improving education; they were eroding it.

What once was a system focused on helping students master foundational skills: phonics, cursive writing, critical thinking, financial literacy, and study strategies, slowly began to change. Decisions were increasingly made for the benefit of districts, universities, and corporate sponsors, rather than for the students sitting in the classrooms. Too often, what was most beneficial for learners was replaced with what was most convenient for institutions.

That realization broke my heart.

Still, I did what I could. Alongside my regular teaching, I created small programs designed to fill in the gaps. I launched a summer program to help middle school students prepare for the challenges of adolescence. I designed after-school programs to strengthen the skills that were often overlooked in the traditional day. I taught summer school and enrichment classes, not just to help struggling students catch up but to give them meaningful new skills that made learning feel alive again.

When I entered the college and university level after twenty years in K–12, I expected to find a higher standard. Instead, I was confronted with a whole new set of challenges. I saw professors who cared deeply about their subjects but showed little interest in their students. I heard colleagues openly declare that certain students "didn't belong" in college. I watched brilliant experts lecture endlessly while their students scrolled through phones, disengaged and discouraged.

The deeper I went, the clearer it became: These professors knew their fields inside and out, but they had never been taught how to teach.

With my background in curriculum and instruction, I couldn't stay silent. I developed and taught a course for college professors and workforce trainers, giving them tools to engage learners and transform classrooms. Over the years, I refined this work into what I now call the TEA4CH™ method, a framework I had practiced for most of my career but which now had the structure, clarity, and evidence to be shared widely.

As I consulted with companies and corporations, I discovered something even more powerful: TEA4CH™ was not confined to schools or universities. It worked just as well in corporate training rooms, workforce development programs, and onboarding initiatives. The method transcended grade levels and institutions because it was never about a single curriculum; it was about how people learn best.

This book is the culmination of those years of discovery, heartbreak, persistence, and hope. It is a call to every teacher, professor, trainer, administrator, and parent. The TEA4CH™ method is not a theory; it is a practical, tested framework that can transform how we prepare learners, not just for jobs and careers but for life.

Education should never be reduced to a diploma hanging on a wall. It must be the catalyst for confidence, critical thinking, and lifelong adaptability. My deepest desire is that *Diploma Deception* will ignite a movement to transform teaching and elevate education so that no student is ever lost, forgotten, or unprepared.

It is time for education to return to its purpose: to equip learners not only to succeed in the workplace but to thrive in life.

Introduction

Why Education Must Change

We hand out diplomas as if they guarantee success. Yet the sobering truth is this: More than half of college graduates (52%) are underemployed within a year of graduation; after ten years, approximately 45% are still working in jobs that do not require a bachelor's degree (Strada Institute & Burning Glass Institute, 2024). Recent data from the New York Federal Reserve confirms the problem, reporting that over 41% of recent graduates are underemployed in 2025 (Federal Reserve Bank of New York, 2025).

Employers echo the concern. A 2025 Deloitte study found that 66% of managers believe their newest hires are not fully prepared for the demands of the workplace (Deloitte, 2025). The gaps are not only technical; they extend to the very professional competencies employers expect from every entry-level employee: communication, adaptability, teamwork, problem-solving, and leadership. Globally, the OECD (2024) has identified the same deficiencies across industries, with firms reporting persistent shortages in collaboration, problem-solving, and resilience.

This is the heart of what I call *Diploma Deception*: the gap between the credentials students receive and the skills they actually need. Degrees look impressive framed on a wall, but too often, they disguise an uncomfortable reality: Graduates are walking into the world unprepared, unsure, and unable to transfer classroom learning into real-world effectiveness.

The Overemphasis on the Credential

We live in a culture that prizes the diploma itself. Students are told from childhood: *Get the degree, and doors will open.* But what happens when those doors stay closed? When the graduate who dutifully paid tuition and completed assignments discovers that employers are more interested in what they can do than what their diploma says?

The result is frustration on both sides. Employers are burdened with training that should have been part of a student's education, and graduates feel cheated, realizing that the paper in their hand doesn't guarantee the confidence or competence they expected.

And yet what pains me most isn't just the economic deception. It's that somewhere along the way, students were never taught *how to think*. Too many are told *what* to think, what to believe, what to memorize, and how to repeat it back. That is not education; it is indoctrination. True education must prepare students to question, to explore, to test, and to discover truth for themselves.

Why Teaching Methods Matter

At the core of this problem lies a deeper issue: how students are taught.

In far too many classrooms, the lecture still reigns supreme. Professors and trainers stand at the front, deliver information, and expect that knowledge to stick. But research shows otherwise: Students in lecture-based courses are 55% more likely to fail compared to those in active learning classrooms (Freeman et al.,

2014). Retention is dismal; students recall only 10–20% of lecture content after just a few days (Bligh, 2000). And inequity widens, as traditional lectures disproportionately harm first-generation and underrepresented students, while active learning cuts achievement gaps by nearly half (Theobald et al., 2020).

Making matters worse, most college professors, trade school instructors, and corporate trainers receive no formal preparation in teaching at all. Unlike K–12 educators who must earn licensure and undergo pedagogical training, higher-ed faculty are often experts in their field but novices in how to engage learners. They lecture on what they know, but few have been taught how to *teach* what they know.

And behind this lack of preparation lurks an even greater danger: I have heard colleagues openly say that students who don't think like they do "don't belong in college." I have seen professors dismiss adult learners and first-generation students as "not worth the time." These words cut deeply because I know what it feels like to struggle until a teacher cared enough to make learning meaningful. Those "students who don't belong"? They are exactly the students who need us most.

A Transformative Alternative: TEA4CH™

That is why I developed the TEA4CH™ method; a simple yet revolutionary approach that shifts education from information delivery to true transformation.

TEA4CH™ transforms learning by focusing on:

- **Teaching:** Provide clear instruction, practical strategies, and live modeling so students don't just hear content, they see how it's done.
- **Example:** Connect learning to real-world stories, case studies, and lived experiences, drawing from what students already know and extending it with new perspectives.
- **Application:** Move from theory to practice through active exercises, action steps, and reflection that cement learning in memory.

And because how an instructor shows up is just as important as what they teach, TEA4CH™ is grounded in four essential habits every effective educator must embody:

1. **Clarity** – Define outcomes, simplify concepts, and eliminate confusion.
2. **Connection** – Build rapport and tie content to students' lives.
3. **Curiosity** – Spark questions, exploration, and critical thinking.
4. **Constant Checks** – Gauge comprehension often and adjust along the way.

Traditional Lecture vs. TEA4CH™

Traditional Lecture	TEA4CH™ Method
<u>Passive Listening</u> – Students sit quietly, take notes, and hope knowledge sticks.	<u>Active Engagement</u> – Students question, discuss, and explore concepts hands-on.
<u>Low Retention</u> – Students recall only 10–20% of lecture content after a few days (Bligh, 2000).	<u>High Retention</u> – Active learning strategies promote long-term mastery and application.
<u>High Failure Rates</u> – Students in lecture-only classes are 55% more likely to fail (Freeman et al., 2014).	<u>Improved Success</u> – Active methods consistently raise test performance and reduce dropout rates.
<u>Widening Inequity</u> – Traditional lectures disproportionately harm underrepresented students (Theobald et al., 2020).	<u>Closing Gaps</u> – TEA4CH™ narrows achievement gaps by nearly 50% through connection and clarity.
<u>Information Delivery</u> – Focused on what the professor knows.	<u>Skill Development</u> – Focused on what students can do with knowledge, problem-solving, communication, and leadership.

Lectures create listeners. TEA4CH™ creates leaders.

More Than the Workplace

When TEA4CH™ is adopted, instructors stop being mere lecturers and start becoming facilitators of transformation. Students don't just walk away with information; they walk away with skills, confidence, and the ability to communicate and adapt in every area of life.

And these skills matter everywhere. The ability to collaborate, to think critically, to solve problems, these aren't just workplace assets, they're life skills, vital in families, communities, and civic life.

The Problem I Couldn't Ignore

After more than thirty-five years in education, I saw this problem firsthand. I sat in classrooms where students' eyes glazed over, not because they didn't care but because no one had engaged them. I watched brilliant professors deliver dazzling research while half their students scrolled on their phones. I spoke with graduates who carried debt and diplomas but confessed, *"I don't feel ready."*

It became clear: Too many instructors were never taught how to teach. That gap was costing students their future and costing society the talent we desperately need.

I spent years developing and teaching a course for new college professors and workforce trainers, testing and refining what worked. Out of that came TEA4CH™, a framework that not only guided educators but also reignited students. When used consistently, it helped learners move beyond memorization into mastery, and beyond dependency into independence.

Reimagining Education Together

This book is more than a critique of what's broken; it's a roadmap for what's possible. My goal isn't simply to expose the deception but to empower educators, students, and institutions to embrace a better way. A way where learning is active, engaging, and transformational. A way where diplomas are no longer empty promises but visible signs of genuine preparation.

If you are an educator, student, parent, or employer who believes we can and must do better, then this book is for you. Together, we can move education from deception to transformation.

Because the truth is this: Education isn't a necessary evil. Education is one of the greatest forces for good—when it teaches students not what to think but how to think so they can discover truth and carry it into every part of their lives.

Part I

The Deception

Chapter One

The Illusion of Success

The Statistic That Should Stop Us in Our Tracks

Walk into almost any college campus, and you'll find students hunched over laptops, juggling assignments, and investing thousands of hours into their education. On the surface, they appear to be preparing for a future of opportunity.

But behind the statistics lies a sobering truth: 45% of college students show no significant improvement in critical thinking, reasoning, or writing skills after two full years of study (Arum & Roksa, 2011).

Two years. Tuition paid. Credits earned. Lectures attended. And yet nearly half of students walk away no better at analyzing information, questioning assumptions, or crafting a persuasive argument than they were when they arrived.

This should stop us in our tracks. If education isn't equipping students with the most fundamental skills of thinking, then what is it doing?

Attendance vs. Engagement

Part of the problem is that diplomas, both in high school and college, measure attendance, not engagement.

- Did you show up?

- Did you complete the assignments?
- Did you accumulate the credits?

If yes, then congratulations: You graduate.

But this focus on time spent rather than skills mastered creates an illusion. A high school diploma says you are "prepared for adulthood." A college degree says you are "ready for a career." Yet, when employers, communities, and families put these assumptions to the test, reality tells a different story.

I saw this constantly in my own classrooms. At the college level, many students believed that simply showing up was enough. If they were present, turned in their work, and passed exams, then they assumed they were learning. But when I required them to engage through discussion, application, or critical thinking, they often pushed back.

Why? Because many of their other classes didn't expect this of them. Those courses reinforced the illusion that presence equaled learning. For some of my students, the first time they were asked to wrestle with questions, analyze perspectives, or apply theory to practice was in my class. It was uncomfortable. Some even asked, *"Why do we need to think this deeply?"*

My answer was simple: *"Why not? This is how you learn best."*

Learning isn't about surviving the course; it's about actively engaging in it.

The Illusion of Success vs. The Reality Employers See

The Illusion of Success	The Reality Employers See
Diploma = Prepared "If you graduate, you're ready for the workforce."	**Credentials ≠ Competence** Only 11% of business leaders strongly agree that graduates are ready (Gallup, 2014).
Attendance = Learning "They were in class, so they must have absorbed the material."	**Minimal Gains in Skills** 45% of students show no improvement in critical thinking after 2 years (Arum & Roksa, 2011).
Ceremony = Achievement "Walking across the stage proves success."	**Employers Disagree** 89% of college leaders say graduates are work-ready, but only 50% of employers agree (Hart Research, 2015).
Degree = Career Ready "A diploma guarantees job opportunities."	**Underemployment Crisis** 52% of grads are underemployed within one year; nearly half are still underemployed 10 years later (Burning Glass Institute, 2022).

A Nation Drifting Away from Skills

It isn't only higher education that is guilty of this drift. As a nation, we have steadily moved away from teaching the kinds of meaningful, practical skills that allow people to thrive no matter their profession.

- **Handwriting:** Once a cornerstone of education, handwriting has been pushed aside in favor of typing. Yet studies show that handwriting improves memory, comprehension, and conceptual understanding because it activates neural pathways differently than typing (Mueller & Oppenheimer, 2014).
- **Personal finance:** Millions graduate without knowing how to budget, save, or manage debt. Surveys reveal that fewer than 1 in 5 students receive formal financial literacy education in high school (Council for Economic Education, 2022).
- **Critical thinking:** A multi-institutional study found that many undergraduates "make only limited gains in critical thinking, reasoning, and writing skills during college" (Arum & Roksa, 2011).
- **Deep reading:** Research shows that "screen reading" habits foster skimming at the expense of comprehension and deep learning (Wolf, 2018).
- **Problem-solving:** Employers consistently rank problem-solving and communication as the top two skills they need yet also the most lacking in new graduates (National Association of Colleges and Employers, 2023).

The absence of these skills is not a minor inconvenience; it's a profound loss. Without them, students face not only career struggles but also personal struggles, financial stress, conflict in relationships, poor decision-making, and a lack of confidence in their ability to adapt.

Skills We Measure vs. Skills That Matter

What Diplomas Measure	What Students Really Need
Credits earned	Ability to think critically
Classes attended	Communication and collaboration skills
Assignments submitted	Problem-solving in real-world contexts
GPA and test scores	Financial literacy and life management
Completion of requirements	Deep reading and sustained focus

Diplomas track compliance. Life demands competence.

The Illusion of Success

This is the illusion of success.

We tell students: *Get the diploma and you'll be set.*

We encourage parents: *If your child walks across the stage, they're ready.*

We assure employers: *Hire graduates and you'll have competent employees.*

But none of these promises are guaranteed. The diploma has become a symbol we revere without asking whether it reflects true growth.

Credentials don't equal competence.

And yet we cling to the illusion because it's easier to celebrate the ceremony than confront the shortcomings. We decorate the diploma, but we neglect the development. We measure credits, but we ignore competencies.

The illusion is comforting. But it's also costly, leaving graduates underprepared, employers frustrated, and society short of the thinkers and problem solvers it needs.

TEA4CH™ Spotlight: Curiosity

The Spark That Ignites Learning

Engagement begins when educators model curiosity and invite questions. Too often, classrooms are built on a one-way flow of information: teacher speaks, students listen. But curiosity changes everything.

When a professor asks, *"I wonder what would happen if...?"* or pauses to explore a question with students, the classroom shifts from passive reception to active discovery.

Curiosity is contagious. It tells students that learning isn't about reciting answers, it's about chasing questions.

I've seen firsthand that when students are given permission to be curious, they come alive. The disengaged student at the back of the room begins to participate. The one who only wanted a grade suddenly wants to learn. The atmosphere shifts.

Without curiosity, we settle for the illusion of success... diplomas that look impressive but hide unpreparedness. With curiosity, we unlock the foundation of all true learning.

The Cost of the Illusion

The consequences of the illusion of success extend far beyond classrooms. Employers spend billions retraining graduates who should have been ready to contribute on day one (Training Industry Report, 2022). Families watch children walk across the stage only to move back home months later, burdened with debt and lacking direction. Communities lose out on the creativity, leadership, and problem-solving that should have been nurtured during a student's education.

One hiring manager put it bluntly: *"We don't need more graduates with diplomas. We need graduates who can think."*

When credentials are mistaken for competence, students are the ones who pay the highest price. They believed the promise. They invested the years. They took on the loans. And they were told that the piece of paper would be the proof of their readiness.

When that proof turns out to be hollow, it's not just an academic failure; it's a betrayal.

A Story Behind the Numbers

Let me share a story. A student, I'll call Maria, was one of the brightest in her class. She graduated with honors, had glowing recommendation letters, and landed a job interview with a company she admired. On paper, she was the model of success.

But when the interviewer asked her to describe a time she had solved a complex problem, she froze. She had memorized formulas, written essays, and aced exams, but she had rarely been asked to apply her knowledge in unpredictable, real-world contexts. The interview ended quickly.

Maria didn't fail because she wasn't intelligent. She failed because her education had given her the illusion of readiness, not the practice of readiness.

Multiply Maria by millions, and you begin to see the scope of the problem.

Setting the Tone for the Journey Ahead

This first chapter isn't meant to discourage. It's meant to reveal the truth we must confront if we want change. The illusion of success is powerful, but it is not permanent.

The rest of this book will peel back the layers of deception and show a better way. We will explore why lectures fall short, why professors aren't taught how to teach, and why students are cheated when education prioritizes credentials over competence. Most importantly, we will explore how the TEA4CH™ method can change this trajectory, replacing illusion with transformation and deception with truth.

Education should not be about creating graduates who look successful. It should be about shaping successful individuals equipped with the thinking, skills, and confidence to thrive in work, life, and community.

That is the journey we are about to take.

CHAPTER TWO

THE SHOCKING TRUTH ABOUT TEACHING

A Statistic That Should Make Us Uncomfortable

Here's a truth that rarely makes headlines: The majority of college professors receive little to no formal training in how to teach. According to the American Council on Education, more than 80% of university faculty are hired primarily for their research expertise, not their teaching ability. In trade schools and corporate training programs, the number is even higher.

This reality has been confirmed time and again. A 2024 analysis noted that in STEM fields especially, professors are chosen and promoted for their research credentials, not for their ability to engage learners (Topaz & Brown, 2024). Similarly, the American Association of University Professors (AAUP) reports that over 68% of U.S. faculty are now in contingent (non-tenure-track) positions, a category that typically offers little to no professional development in pedagogy (AAUP, 2023).

Think about that for a moment. To teach in a K–12 classroom, teachers must complete coursework in pedagogy, pass licensing exams, and undergo supervised practice. Yet in higher education, the very place entrusted with preparing adults for professional life, professors are often handed a syllabus and told to "figure it out."

The shocking truth is that expertise in a subject does not equal expertise in teaching that subject. And the people paying the price are students.

When Knowledge Isn't Enough

Consider this scenario: A chemistry professor has spent decades studying molecular interactions. Their research is brilliant. Their publications are impressive. They are a recognized expert in their field. But when they step into the classroom, the brilliance stops translating. They deliver long lectures in a monotone voice, scribble equations on the board without explanation, and dismiss student questions as "basic."

The result? Students walk away frustrated, confused, and convinced that chemistry is impossible to understand.

The tragedy isn't a lack of passion for chemistry. This professor is deeply passionate about the science. But passion for the subject is not the same as passion for the student. Professors are rewarded for publishing, for securing grants, and for building a reputation in their discipline. Their career depends on producing research, not producing understanding in the minds of students.

And so, in practice, teaching becomes secondary. The lecture is less about connecting with learners and more about affirming the professor's expertise. The classroom turns into a stage for authority rather than a space for discovery.

Research confirms this disconnect. Studies show that when students passively listen to lectures, retention drops from about 70% immediately after a class to as little as 10% just a few days later

(CTSNet, 2022). Without strategies to engage, illustrate, and invite participation, most of the knowledge professors hope to transfer evaporates almost instantly. Students don't just fail to learn; they internalize the belief that the failure is their own, that they simply aren't smart enough, when in , the system was never designed to help them succeed.

But now consider a different professor. This one also knows chemistry inside and out. Their research record is solid. But when they step into the classroom, something changes. They pause to tell a story about how a discovery was made, they compare molecular bonds to the snap of Velcro, they stop mid-equation to check for understanding. They invite questions, especially the "basic" ones, because they know those are the real starting points of learning. Their students don't just memorize reactions; they begin to see chemistry as a puzzle they can actually solve.

Two professors, same knowledge. One leaves students lost. The other leaves students inspired.

The difference? One relies on expertise alone. The other knows that knowledge must be translated into clarity, connection, and curiosity. That doesn't happen by accident; it happens through a deliberate method of teaching. A method that not only delivers information but transforms it into understanding.

From Knowledge to Transformation: Enter TEA/TEA4CH™

If knowledge alone isn't enough, then what is?

The answer lies in how that knowledge is communicated, received, and applied. Teaching isn't just about passing information from one mind to another, it's about creating transformation in the learner. That transformation happens only when students can grasp the concept, see it in action, and practice it themselves.

That's why I developed the TEA Method—**Teaching, Example, Application.** It's simple in design but powerful in impact.

- **Teaching provides clarity.** It breaks down the concept in ways students can understand, using language that connects rather than intimidates.
- **Example provides connection.** It shows the idea in action through story, analogy, and demonstration so learners see not just what it is but how it works.
- **Application provides curiosity and confidence.** It gives students the chance to try it themselves, to wrestle with the material, and to discover they can do it.

When these three steps are present, learning sticks. Students don't just hear the material; they own it.

But the TEA Method alone isn't enough in a system where teachers face competing demands, outdated expectations, and students with wildly different learning needs. That's why I expanded it into **TEA4CH™**, a framework that takes the core of TEA and strengthens it with four essentials every teacher needs: **Clarity, Connection, Curiosity, and Checks.**

This framework doesn't ask teachers to abandon their expertise. Instead, it equips them to translate expertise into transformation. It gives them a process for ensuring that knowledge becomes understanding, that lectures become conversations, and that classrooms become places of discovery instead of despair.

Because the truth is this: The best professors and teachers aren't the ones who know the most. They're the ones who can help students believe they can know more, do more, and become more.

A Case Study

Chemistry Reimagined Through TEA/TEA4CH™

Let's return to the chemistry classroom. Same subject. Same complex molecular concepts. But now, let's watch what happens when the professor teaches using TEA/TEA4CH™.

- **Teaching (Clarity):** Instead of diving straight into equations, the professor begins with a simple explanation: "Molecules are like people at a party. Some pair off quickly, some drift apart, and some need a little push to connect." The intimidating chemical language is replaced with an entry point that students can immediately understand.
- **Example (Connection):** To bring it to life, the professor shows a short video of magnets snapping together and then compares that to ionic bonds. They draw a parallel between Velcro strips and covalent bonds. Suddenly, abstract terms aren't abstract anymore; they're connected to everyday experience.
- **Application (Curiosity + Confidence):** Students are handed small sets of Lego blocks. Their task is to build different "molecules" using rules for bonding. In minutes, they're laughing, experimenting, and explaining bonding patterns

to each other. The concepts that once seemed impossible are now tangible.
- **Clarity, Connection, Curiosity, Checks:** As the activity ends, the professor checks understanding by asking students to explain, in their own words, how their Lego "molecule" compares to a real chemical bond. Misconceptions are caught early, corrected on the spot, and celebrated as part of learning.

The result? Instead of glazed eyes and frantic note-taking, there's curiosity, discussion, and even joy. Students walk away not just knowing chemistry facts but understanding chemistry as a living system they can work with.

And this isn't just a nice story; it's backed by evidence. A landmark 2014 study in the *Proceedings of the National Academy of Sciences* found that students in active learning classrooms performed half a letter grade higher on average and were 1.5 times less likely to fail compared to those in traditional lecture-only courses (Freeman et al., 2014). In other words, when students are engaged through methods like TEA/TEA4CH™, not only do they learn more, they also succeed more.

The Student Experience

If you ask students about their most memorable teachers, they rarely say, "She was brilliant at research" or "He published in the top journals." They say things like:

- "She made complicated things simple."

- "He cared enough to explain it three different ways until I got it."
- "She connected the subject to my life."

These aren't marks of subject expertise. They're marks of teaching skill.

And yet countless students spend thousands of dollars sitting through lectures that do little more than recite information. They leave the classroom knowing what their professors know but not knowing what to do with it.

TEA4CH™ Spotlight

Clarity – The Foundation of Learning

Confusion is the enemy of engagement. Clarity begins when educators define learning goals, explain concepts in simple language, and eliminate unnecessary complexity. A clear teacher doesn't "dumb down" content; instead, they open it up.

Clarity means saying, *"By the end of today's lesson, you will be able to…"* It means breaking information into digestible steps. It means checking for understanding before moving on.

When students are clear about what they're learning and why, they lean in. When they're confused, they check out.

The Cost of Unclear Teaching

When professors aren't trained to teach clearly, students pay in multiple ways:

- **Financial cost:** Courses must be retaken, adding thousands in tuition and fees.
- **Emotional cost:** Students blame themselves for not "getting it," when in fact the teaching was unclear.
- **Professional cost:** Graduates leave with shaky foundations, which leads to difficulties in applying knowledge on the job and reflects negatively on the institution they attended.

This is why so many graduates feel like impostors in the workplace. They passed exams, but they never fully grasped the concepts.

A Story Behind the Truth

I once observed a new professor, let's call him Dr. Lee, teaching a business course. He was brilliant in finance, a successful consultant, and highly respected in his field. But his lecture was a flood of jargon and slides crammed with text. Half the students sat silently, overwhelmed.

During a break, I asked one of the students what she thought. She said, *"I know he's smart. But I have no idea what he wants us to learn."*

That single comment sums up the problem. Students don't just need access to expert knowledge. They need clarity, a roadmap that helps them understand, connect, and apply that knowledge.

From Truth to Transformation

The shocking truth is that most professors aren't trained to teach. But the hopeful truth is that this can change. Teaching isn't an inborn talent; it's a skill that can be developed. And clarity is the first step.

Imagine the impact if every professor, trainer, and educator paused before each class to ask three simple questions:

- *What do I want my students to know, feel, and do by the end of this lesson?*
- *How can I explain this concept in the simplest, most accessible way?*
- *How will I know they understand before I move on?*

If professors embraced these questions, classrooms would be transformed overnight, more than by any new technology or trendy teaching tool.

And yet, in my tenure at the college and university level, I witnessed a sobering reality: Only a small percentage of professors knew how to teach, much less cared about learning how. Some who were required to take my course on effective teaching refused to show up, insisting, *"I know my subject. That should be enough. Otherwise, I wouldn't have been hired."*

But here lies the problem: Knowing a subject is not the same as teaching it. Expertise alone doesn't equal effectiveness.

Colleges and universities owe it to students and to the parents who invest tens of thousands of dollars in tuition to ensure professors know how to teach, not just research and publish. If publishing is truly the higher priority, then let's stop calling these institutions places of learning and start calling them what they are: research institutions.

But students and parents aren't paying for research alone. They're paying for an education. They deserve professors who are as committed to teaching as they are to their fields of study.

This isn't a call out. It's a call to. Professors, you have the opportunity to change the trajectory of your students' lives, not just by delivering content but by teaching them how to think, how to question, and how to apply knowledge in meaningful ways.

And colleges and universities, you, too, must rise higher. Hold your faculty accountable. Make pedagogy a priority. Provide training, demand engagement, and reward excellence in teaching, not only in publishing.

Because at the end of the day, students and parents deserve the truth: Higher education isn't just about collecting diplomas but about equipping learners with skills for work, life, and leadership. Anything less is deception.

Setting the Stage for What's Next

Clarity is only the beginning. Once we help students see what they're learning and why, we must also rethink how we are teaching it. Which brings us to the next chapter: the lecture. For centuries, it has been the default mode of instruction. But does it actually work? Or is it part of the deception that keeps students passive and unprepared?

That's where we'll go next.

Chapter Three

Why Lecture Fails

The Statistic We Can't Ignore

For centuries, the lecture has been the dominant form of teaching in higher education. Picture the scene: rows of students in fixed seats, a professor at the front speaking for an hour, and students scribbling notes furiously. It's a tradition older than most of our universities.

But here's the problem: Students retain, on average, only 10% of what they hear in a lecture within forty-eight hours. After a week, most of it is gone (Bligh, 2000).

If this were a medical treatment, it would never pass clinical trials. If it were a business practice, it would bankrupt the company. Yet, in education, the lecture remains the gold standard.

The Myth of the "Good Lecture"

Defenders of lecture often say, *"But I had a professor who gave amazing lectures."* And it's true, some lecturers are riveting. They tell stories, they inspire, they keep students awake with humor or passion.

But even then, research shows that retention is minimal compared to active learning. A lecture, no matter how brilliant, is still passive. Students are observers, not participants. They might leave entertained or even inspired, but inspiration without application fades quickly.

The myth of the "good lecture" is one of education's most persistent deceptions.

What Students Really Experience

Ask students what lecture-based classes feel like, and you'll hear:

- *"I zone out after the first 15 minutes."*
- *"I can memorize the slides, but I don't really get it."*
- *"If I miss a lecture, I feel completely lost."*

This isn't laziness. It's human nature. Our brains aren't designed to absorb and retain hours of unbroken information. Without interaction, questioning, or practice, information simply slips away.

I saw this repeatedly in my own teaching career. Students would come into my class after years of being conditioned to sit silently and absorb. They thought this was enough. But when I pushed them to engage, to question, to apply, to think, they often struggled. Not because they lacked ability but because lectures had never prepared them for what real learning demanded.

The Passive Problem

Here's the core issue: Lecture creates passive learners.

- The teacher does the talking.
- The slides do the explaining.
- The student does the sitting.

Passive learning rewards compliance, not curiosity. It trains students to listen quietly, take notes, and repeat information on exams but not to think critically, problem-solve, or apply knowledge in dynamic ways.

And when students graduate into a world that demands adaptability, creativity, and communication, they are unprepared.

TEA4CH™ Spotlight: Teaching

The Core of the Framework

Teaching: More Than Telling

Teaching isn't about delivering information; it's about guiding transformation. The best teaching is intentional: it provides clear instruction, models the process, and offers strategies students can replicate.

In TEA4CH™, *Teaching* is the beating heart of the method. It's where information becomes transformation. It means moving beyond *"Here's what I know"* to *"Here's how you can know and do it too."*

It means:

- Modeling: demonstrating how to think, solve, or create in real time.
- Strategies: giving students practical tools they can use beyond the classroom.
- Scaffolding: breaking down complexity into manageable steps so confidence grows alongside competence.

This is where higher education has lost its way. Students spend twelve years in K–12 classrooms where (at least at best) they are guided, supported, and given ways to practice. Then, suddenly, in college, many are thrown into a model where they are expected to sit, listen, and absorb for hours at a time. This isn't preparation; it's regression.

I saw professors who believed lecturing was synonymous with teaching. One told me flatly, *"My job is to deliver the content. What they do with it is up to them."* But this is not teaching, it's transmitting. It's no different than attending a motivational speech: you may leave inspired, but a week later, you've forgotten the details unless you had to cram them for an exam.

Real teaching equips students with behaviors, strategies, and experiences they can carry into careers and life. That's the TEA4CH™ difference.

A Tale of Two Classrooms

Consider two history classes covering the same material:

- Classroom A: The professor lectures for an hour on the causes of the Civil War. Students take notes, highlight their textbooks, and prepare for a multiple-choice exam.
- Classroom B: The professor introduces the same causes, then divides students into groups to role-play debates from the 1860s. One group argues from the perspective of Southern landowners, another from Northern industrialists, another from enslaved individuals seeking freedom. Students must prepare their arguments, present, and respond to challenges.

Which students will remember the material longer? Which will be able to apply critical thinking, communication, and empathy beyond the classroom?

The answer is obvious. Classroom B creates engaged learners who are practicing real skills, not just memorizing facts.

The Hidden Cost of Lectures

When institutions cling to lectures, the cost is profound and well-documented.

- **Retention suffers.** Students may listen intently, even take careful notes, but the reality is sobering: Studies show that students retain only 10–20% of lecture material after just a few days (Bligh, 2000). What's worse, they must relearn the same content repeatedly, creating a cycle of shallow understanding rather than lasting knowledge.
- **Engagement collapses.** A landmark meta-analysis revealed that students in traditional lecture-based courses were 55% more likely to fail than those in active learning environments (Freeman et al., 2014). Put bluntly, lectures don't just bore students; they set them up for failure.
- **Inequity deepens.** Traditional lectures are not neutral. They privilege students who already have background knowledge or resources like tutors, while those without such support fall further behind. Active learning, by contrast, has been shown to cut achievement gaps for underrepresented students by nearly half (Theobald et al., 2020).

The lecture doesn't merely fail to deliver; it amplifies disadvantage. It creates a classroom where only some succeed, and too many fail. And it does so not because students lack ability, but because the method itself is outdated, inequitable, and ineffective.

The Employer's Perspective

Employers consistently report that graduates lack critical workplace skills like communication, teamwork, and problem-solving. Why? Because lectures don't build these skills. Listening to a professor talk about communication is not the same as practicing it.

Recent employer surveys highlight this gap clearly. In a 2023 report, the National Association of Colleges and Employers (NACE) ranked the top skills employers seek: problem-solving, teamwork, communication, and adaptability. Yet those same employers noted these were the very areas where graduates fell short (NACE, 2023). The Association of American Colleges & Universities found similar results: while 89% of college leaders believed their students were prepared for work, only 50% of employers agreed (Hart Research Associates, 2015).

An executive once put it bluntly: *"I don't hire people to sit quietly and take notes. I hire people who can think on their feet, challenge assumptions, and solve problems."*

And here's the truth: lectures don't build those muscles. They train compliance, not curiosity. They produce note-takers, not problem-solvers.

From Lecture to Learning

This is not to say that lectures must disappear entirely. Short, targeted explanations have their place. But a lecture should never be the backbone of education. It should be the springboard for active engagement.

Imagine a classroom where the professor spends ten minutes introducing a concept, then guides students in applying it through discussion, simulation, or practice. Suddenly, students aren't just listeners, they're participants.

That is teaching.

Looking Ahead

Lecture is the symbol of education's past. Connection is the symbol of its future. If students are to succeed, we must move from broadcasting information to building relationships.

That brings us to the next chapter: what students really need and why connection is the missing ingredient that makes learning personal, meaningful, and unforgettable.

Chapter Four

What Students Really Need

The Statistic That Says It All

Employers are sounding the alarm: Graduates may hold diplomas, but too often they lack the skills that matter most in the workplace. A national survey by the Association of American Colleges & Universities (AAC&U) found that 70% of employers believe graduates are underprepared in critical areas like communication, teamwork, and problem-solving (AAC&U, 2021).

The gap isn't about intelligence or effort, it's about a system that prizes credentials over connection. Employers don't just want students who can pass exams; they want students who can connect with ideas, with people, and with real-world challenges.

And the students themselves know it. A 2025 Hult International Business School survey reported that 77% of recent graduates felt they learned more in the first six months on the job than in their entire undergraduate education, while only 24% felt fully prepared for their roles (Hult, 2025).

The Human Side of Learning

When you think back to the teachers who made the biggest impact on your life, you likely don't remember their test questions or grading rubrics. You remember how they made you feel:

- The teacher who looked you in the eye and said, *"I believe in you."*
- The professor who patiently explained something until it finally clicked.
- The mentor who connected the lesson to your life outside the classroom.

Why do those memories endure? Because connection transforms learning.

"Students don't care how much you know until they know how much you care."

~ Anonymous

As John Dewey observed: "A teacher's quality is determined by their ability to respond to the movement of the student's mind… they appreciate their difficulties, entering into their problems, sharing their intellectual victories." (Dewey, *Democracy and Education*, 1916)

Connection, then, is not sentimental. It is foundational.

The Deception: Success Without Connection

Here's the deception: we've convinced ourselves that if students absorb content, they are educated. But content without connection is fragile. It doesn't last. It doesn't transfer. It doesn't change behavior.

Think of the countless students who sat through lectures, earned passing grades, and yet left with no passion for the subject and no confidence in themselves. They were taught information, but they weren't taught in a way that connected to who they are and what they care about.

That isn't success. That's survival.

TEA4CH™ Spotlight: Connection

With TEA4CH™, connection transforms classrooms from places of information into communities of transformation.

Connection: Making Learning Personal

Connection isn't an "extra" in education; it's the difference between compliance and engagement, between survival and transformation.

Why Connection Matters

- **Motivation & Engagement**: Students with strong teacher–student relationships show higher motivation, stronger social skills, and fewer behavioral problems (American Psychological Association, 2022).
- **Belonging & Persistence**: Students who feel connected to at least one professor are twice as likely to persist to graduation (NSSE, 2021).
- **Memory & Retention**: Emotions act as "gatekeepers" to memory; students remember best when content is tied to human connection (Immordino-Yang & Damasio, 2007).
- **Employability**: Employers stress that they can train technical systems but cannot easily train adaptability, collaboration, and communication (Hult, 2025).

Connection in Practice — Research + Real Lives

1. Relationships Drive Engagement

- **Research**: Gallup's national survey found that students who strongly agreed *"my teacher cares about me as a person"* were 2.5 times more likely to be engaged in school (Gallup, 2018).
- **Sylvia's Story**: Sylvia was a recently divorced mother of ten children, taking just one class to begin her academic career. She was an excellent student but often overwhelmed. Many times, she would stay, in tears, after class, convinced she had to give up her dream of entering the medical field. On several occasions, we sat together, breaking down her assignments into manageable pieces and discussing how to juggle responsibilities at home. That added time helped her gain confidence. She not only succeeded in the class but also went on to graduate from community college and pursue a nursing degree. What turned the tide wasn't just academics; it was connection.

2. Emotional Connection Fuels Memory

- **Research**: Neuroscience shows that emotional relevance is essential for deep learning (Immordino-Yang & Damasio, 2007).
- **Jose's Story**: Jose worked nights to support his younger siblings. He was bright but disengaged, his energy drained by survival. I asked him to connect an economics lesson on scarcity to his lived experience. He shared how budgeting

groceries taught him tough trade-offs. Suddenly, the abstract concept was personal and unforgettable. From then on, he leaned in, contributing insights with confidence.

3. Positive Relationships Predict Achievement

- **Research**: A meta-analysis of 119 studies concluded that positive teacher–student relationships strongly predict higher GPAs and test scores (Cornelius-White, 2007).
- **Mason's Story**: Mason sat in the back row, silent and withdrawn. One day, I asked about his part-time job. His face lit up as he described solving a customer-service problem, and we linked it to our lesson on problem-solving. That single moment unlocked his voice. For the rest of the semester, he contributed sharp insights and grew into one of the strongest performers in the class.

4. Connection Builds Belonging & Persistence

- **Research**: The National Survey of Student Engagement found that connection predicts persistence and graduation rates (NSSE, 2021).
- **Julie's Story**: At a trade school, Julie confided that she was the first in her family to pursue certification. She doubted she belonged. I made a point of calling on her for small wins: "That's a great insight, Julie." Over time, her confidence grew. By the semester's end, she was mentoring peers and signing up for advanced courses. Connection fostered belonging, and belonging sustained her success.

What Connection Looks Like in Action

1. **Personal Stories First**
   - Invite students' lived experiences before introducing theory. When a math lesson begins with a story about managing a household budget, or a history class opens by asking, *"What's the biggest change you've seen in your lifetime?"*, students lean in. Their stories give the lesson a personal anchor.

2. **Real-World Anchors**
   - Tie lessons to issues in their communities. A science teacher who connects climate data to a local drought, or a business instructor who links marketing principles to a student's part-time job, turns abstract content into urgent, relevant learning.

3. **Micro-Connections Daily**
   - Connection isn't just the big moments; it's the small, steady signals that say, *"I see you."* Greeting students by name, noticing when someone seems discouraged, or celebrating a small academic win builds trust over time. These micro-connections create the foundation for resilience.

4. **Teacher Transparency**
   - Students connect more deeply when they know their teacher is human, too. Sharing your own struggles, *"I remember failing my first exam and thinking I wasn't cut out for this,"* gives students permission to persist through failure. Vulnerability creates a bridge that pure expertise cannot.

Closing Tie-In:

Connection doesn't require grand gestures; it thrives in consistent practice. When teachers weave stories, real-world relevance, daily recognition, and transparency into their classrooms, students stop feeling like passive receivers of information and start seeing themselves as active participants in learning and in their own futures.

Connection in the TEA4CH™ Framework

- **Teaching**: Shifts from "delivering content" to "teaching humans."
- **Example**: Modeling empathy and respect in every interaction.
- **Application**: Giving students chances to apply knowledge to *their own lives.*

The 4CH Behaviors reinforce it:

- **Clarity** – Students connect only with what they understand.
- **Connection** – The heart of learning, not an accessory.
- **Curiosity** – Ask questions that invite students into discovery.
- **Checks** – Use feedback loops that affirm and guide.

A Tale of Two Professors

- **Professor A**: delivers polished lectures with accurate content. Students take notes, take tests, and walk away unchanged.

- **Professor B**: begins class by asking what students already know, shares her own stories, invites discussion, and ties theory to practice. Students feel seen and valued. They walk away transformed.

Both know their subject. Only one knows their students.

What Students Are Saying

Students describe meaningful learning moments in human, not academic terms:

- *"That was the first time I felt like someone understood how hard this was for me."*
- *"I finally saw why this subject matters in my future."*
- *"He made me feel like my ideas were worth sharing."*

Ironically, these human outcomes drive the strongest academic results. Connected students are motivated students. Motivated students are successful students.

The Employer's Frustration

Employers echo what students already know: Technical knowledge alone is not enough. As one manager put it, *"I can teach new hires our systems. What I can't teach is curiosity, adaptability, or how to collaborate."*

- In Australia, studies show up to 90% of technically qualified applicants lack employability skills like communication and teamwork (Jobs and Skills Australia, 2024).

- In the UK, only 3% of managers believe graduates are fully work-ready (The Times, 2024).
- In the U.S., just 49% of employers say graduates are very prepared in oral communication (Higher Ed Dive, 2023).

The skills employers most value… teamwork, adaptability, and emotional intelligence—precisely those nurtured in classrooms where *connection* is prioritized.

The Power of Connection in Practice

Sometimes the difference between disengagement and transformation is simply this: a teacher who takes time to connect.

Professor Without Connection

Professor Carter walks into class, opens his slides, and dives directly into the material. His explanations are accurate, his outlines are organized, but he rarely looks up. Questions go unasked because students don't feel comfortable interrupting. Assignments are returned with a grade and little else. At the end of the semester, most students pass the exam, but few remember much beyond the test date. Several leave the course doubting their ability in the subject, convinced they just "aren't good at it."

Professor With Connection

Professor Reyes begins each class with a question: *"What's something you noticed this week that ties into our topic?"* She learns her students' names and notices when one is struggling. When Jason, the quiet back-row student, barely participates, she asks about his part-time job and suddenly connects the day's lesson to his customer service experience. When Sylvia, a single mom juggling ten children and coursework, feels overwhelmed, Professor Reyes takes time after class to break assignments into smaller steps, encouraging her that she belongs in the program. Assignments come back with personalized feedback that highlights strengths as well as growth. By the end of the semester, students don't just pass; they see themselves as capable learners. Jason finds his voice. Sylvia pursues her nursing degree.

The Results

- **Without Connection**: Students walk away with content but little confidence, knowledge but no sense of direction. Learning is mechanical, short-lived, and uninspiring.
- **With Connection**: Students carry forward both knowledge and purpose. They are more engaged, more resilient, and more prepared for life beyond the classroom.

Closing Tie-In:

Connection isn't an extra. It is the bridge between knowledge and purpose, between classroom learning and lifelong growth. When teachers choose connection, they don't just teach a subject; they shape a student's future.

What Students Really Need

Students don't just need more information, they need connection. They need teachers who:

- See them as individuals, not just names on a roster.

- Link lessons to their lives, not just a textbook.
- Connect knowledge to purpose.

Because without connection, students may graduate with diplomas but not with direction.

Looking Ahead

We've seen that clarity makes learning possible, and teaching makes it practical. But connection makes it personal, and without it, education fails to inspire.

Still, connection alone isn't enough. Students also need to see how knowledge is lived out in the real world. That brings us to the next chapter: Real-World vs. Classroom, where we'll explore why examples, stories, and case studies matter more than memorization.

Chapter Five

Real-World vs. Classroom

The Statistic That Speaks Volumes

Numbers don't lie. They tell a story the education system often avoids. A recent national survey of U.S. hiring managers reported that eight in ten said at least one recent college graduate they hired in the past year "didn't work out," and 65% said they had to fire a recent graduate within the first year (Resume.org, 2025). Even more sobering, only 58% of companies said they would consider hiring from the Class of 2025 (National Association of Colleges and Employers [NACE], 2025).

Broader employer reporting mirrors this concern: Over half of hiring managers describe recent graduates as unprepared for the workforce, citing issues such as excessive phone use, lack of professionalism, and weak time management (HR Dive, 2025). The message is clear: The diploma may certify knowledge, but employers are questioning its weight as proof of readiness. Students may leave school with high GPAs and glowing transcripts yet falter when asked to solve problems, adapt under pressure, manage time, or navigate workplace dynamics.

Employer priorities are consistent: Problem-solving, teamwork, communication, and initiative top the list, yet employers rate new graduates as under-proficient in exactly these areas (NACE, 2024; NACE, 2025). Practical experience also matters: Paid internships, apprenticeships, and work-based learning are strongly correlated with higher early-career wages and better hiring outcomes (Strada Education Foundation, 2023).

This gap isn't rooted in laziness or lack of potential; it's in how students were trained. Too much of learning is confined to tidy classrooms, neat assignments, and predictable tests. The real world is messy, complex, and unscripted. Without preparation in that space, students step into jobs unready for the unpredictability ahead.

The Deception: Knowledge Without Context

Education has long sold a false promise: If students "know enough," they will naturally succeed in practice. The assumption is seductive but flawed. Knowledge without context is brittle. It looks impressive on paper but cracks under the first stress test of reality.

Consider these everyday scenarios:

- A student who can recite the quadratic formula but freezes when asked to apply it to a business profit-margin scenario.
- A nursing graduate who aced anatomy but panics when a patient's symptoms don't match the textbook description.
- A new employee who memorized company policies but can't navigate a tense client meeting.

What these situations reveal is simple: Classrooms often produce content-ready graduates, but the world needs competence-ready professionals.

What Employers See

When employers talk about today's graduates, their frustrations echo across industries:

- "When the client raised an issue that wasn't in the training manual, our new hire shut down completely. She could quote policies word for word but couldn't improvise a solution."
- "We had a graduate who could solve equations on paper but couldn't figure out why a machine was overheating. Real problems don't come with step-by-step instructions."
- "We don't mind teaching company-specific systems, but we're having to start with basics like communication, time management, and teamwork. That's not what we expect from a four-year degree."
- "Bright grads ace technical assessments, but the moment something unpredictable happens, they're paralyzed. We spend months retraining them just to handle reality."

These aren't isolated complaints. In NACE's surveys, problem-solving and teamwork consistently top the list of attributes employers seek on résumés, with written communication and work ethic close behind. Yet fewer than 55% of employers rate new graduates as proficient in these same areas, even while students overestimate their own skills (NACE, 2025).

This isn't just anecdotal frustration; it's a systemic indictment of an education system that prioritizes information transfer over skill formation.

TEA4CH™ Spotlight: Example

With TEA4CH™, the lesson doesn't end at theory; it begins with the example.

In the TEA4CH™ model, E = Example, and it is one of the most powerful teaching tools we have. Without examples, theory floats in the abstract. With examples, knowledge finds its anchor. Students no longer ask, "When will I ever use this?" because they've already used it.

Why Examples Matter

- Context creates clarity.
- Examples build mental models, much like a toolbox ready for unexpected repairs.
- Stories stick. Humans remember stories up to 22 times more than isolated facts.

Example in TEA4CH™ Practice

- **Case Studies:** Ethics students analyze a real corporate scandal and wrestle with the gray areas, not just definitions.
- **Lived Experiences:** A student's after-school job becomes the dataset for statistics, making formulas practical.
- **Storytelling + Simulation:** A nursing instructor narrates an emergency scenario, then runs a simulation; students debrief decisions.

Without Example: Supply and demand end with a neat graph.

With Example: Students run pop-up "businesses" where survival depends on adjusting prices, supply, and response to shocks.

Trade Schools: Building Real Skills Real Fast

While traditional education often gets stuck in the content bubble, trade schools provide a compelling counterexample. They start with the premise that learning must connect directly to practice. A welder, electrician, or medical imaging specialist doesn't just learn the theory; every lesson includes hands-on application.

Evidence backs this approach:

- Career Academies show sustained earnings gains of about 11% more per year over eight years, without harming academic outcomes (Kemple & Willner, 2008).
- Community College Career and Technical Education (CTE) programs yield higher wages and improved employment status, even for students who don't complete a degree (Pham, Greaney, & Abel, 2020).
- Apprenticeships cluster in high-wage, high-growth occupations, with mean hourly wages above the U.S. average (Bureau of Labor Statistics, 2024).

Where TEA4CH™ enhances trade training:

- Teaching = modeling step-by-step demonstrations.
- Example = connecting procedures to real jobsites.
- Application = immediate, repeated practice.

- Clarity = explicit performance criteria.
- Connection = linking to teamwork and customer expectations.
- Curiosity = troubleshooting failures.
- Checks = frequent skill verifications with immediate feedback.

The result: graduates who can step in on day one and contribute. Which is exactly what employers say they need (American Institutes for Research, 2024).

A Tale of Two Trainers

- **Trainer, Theory Only:** walks through the "five steps of handling a complaint," hands out a checklist, and schedules a quiz.
- **Trainer, Real-World:** covers the same five steps but runs a live role-play with a surprise twist. Students must adapt in real time, then debrief what worked and what didn't.

Both deliver content. Only one builds competence under pressure.

When Examples Unlock Understanding

I once worked with a student, call her *Mia*, who struggled in statistics. She could recite formulas but froze when asked to apply them. One day, we used her retail job as the context. Together, we crunched her store's sales data to calculate trends. Suddenly, statistics came alive. They weren't abstract anymore; they answered questions she cared about: *Which products sell best? What months are busiest?*

Mia's confidence transformed. She went from memorizing equations to interpreting information she could act on. That's what happens when theory is anchored in an example that matters.

The Student Voice

Students say it again and again:
- "I didn't understand it until we did the case study."
- "The story made it click for me."
- "Now I see how I can actually use this."

Students don't want less theory. They want theory that leads somewhere. Examples don't water down learning; they enrich it.

Why Real-World Learning Matters

The stakes are high. Without real-world examples, students become passive collectors of information. With examples, they become flexible problem-solvers and adaptable thinkers.

Life doesn't hand out multiple-choice tests. It hands out complex problems, conflicting interests, and unpredictable outcomes. If education doesn't prepare students for that, it fails its mission.

And the labor market rewards this shift: Paid internships, apprenticeships, and work-based learning consistently improve wages, employment rates, and long-term outcomes (Strada Education Foundation, 2023; GAO, 2025).

A Manager's Story

A hiring manager told me about a graduate who breezed through technical assessments but froze in front of a client: "She knew the formulas, but when the conversation went off script, she panicked. It was like she'd never been trained to think on her feet."

What that graduate lacked wasn't intelligence. It was exposure. Without scenarios that mimic real-world unpredictability, she had no mental map for how to adapt. Examples, especially those embedded in guided practice, build that adaptability.

What Students Really Need

Students don't just need to know more; they need to become more. They need theories that meet reality, knowledge that matures into wisdom, and practice that builds competence.

In the end, students don't graduate into classrooms. They graduate into life. And life requires more than memorization. It requires application, adaptability, and resilience, the very qualities TEA4CH™ cultivates.

Looking Ahead

So far, we've explored curiosity, clarity, connection, and the power of example. But even with examples, learning collapses without one final ingredient: feedback. The next chapter explores the missing feedback loop... why grades aren't enough, why silence stunts growth, and why constant checks are the lifeline of real learning.

Chapter Six

The Missing Feedback Loop

The Statistic That Reveals the Gap

Educational research has consistently shown that students who receive frequent feedback learn at nearly double the rate of those who receive only end-of-unit grades. John Hattie's landmark synthesis of over eight hundred meta-analyses ranked feedback as one of the top five most powerful influences on student achievement, with an effect size greater than many structural reforms (Hattie, 2009). More recently, a meta-analysis of over 435 studies reconfirmed that the power of feedback remains among the strongest educational interventions, with effectiveness amplified when it is specific, actionable, and timely (Wisniewski, Zierer, & Hattie, 2020).

And yet, in too many classrooms, the primary form of "feedback" is still a grade, delivered days or even weeks after the assignment is completed. By then, the moment for correction and growth has passed.

This is the missing feedback loop. Without it, education becomes a guessing game. Students operate in the dark, unsure whether their approach is right until it's too late to adjust, and then at that point, it's no longer relevant.

The Deception: Grades Are Enough

Grades masquerade as feedback, but they're not. A grade is a judgment, not guidance.

- An A says, "You did well." But it doesn't explain why.
- A C says, "You're struggling." But it doesn't show how to improve.
- An F says, "You failed." But it doesn't offer a way forward.

Black and Wiliam's research (1998) demonstrated that grades alone often depress learning because students interpret them as labels. In contrast, narrative comments that explain strengths and outline improvements dramatically increase both motivation and achievement.

More recent findings echo this. In a large-scale analysis of automated writing feedback, effect sizes showed significant improvement in student performance ($g \approx 0.55$) when feedback was immediate and detailed (Fleckenstein et al., 2023). This demonstrates that students don't need to wait for weeks for meaningful input; timely and practical guidance is what accelerates growth.

The Student Perspective

Ask students about grades, and their frustration is clear:

- "By the time I got my paper back, we had already moved on to the next topic."
- "I knew I did something wrong, but I didn't know what or how to fix it."
- "I just looked at the grade and tossed the paper aside."

Grades may spark a moment of pride or disappointment, but they rarely teach. What teaches is feedback… specific, meaningful, timely, and actionable.

TEA4CH™ Spotlight: Constant Checks

In TEA4CH™, constant checks aren't interruptions; they're the heartbeat of learning.

Feedback in TEA4CH™ takes the form of Constant Checks. These are not grand assessments or high-stakes events. They are the small, steady signals that tell students: *You're on track here. Adjust here. Try this next time.*

What Constant Checks Look Like

- Asking a quick mid-lesson question to gauge comprehension.
- Using "exit tickets" where students jot down one thing they learned and one thing they still don't understand.
- Giving short, targeted comments on drafts or assignments that tell students both what they did well and what to adjust.
- Encouraging peer-to-peer feedback and guided self-reflection.

Why Constant Checks Matter

Timely feedback has four times the impact on learning compared to delayed feedback (Wisniewski, Zierer, & Hattie, 2020).

When students understand their missteps quickly, they can immediately course-correct. The loop stays alive.

The message behind every constant check is: *"I'm not here to judge you. I'm here to help you grow and learn."*

A Tale of Two Teachers

- **Teacher A** hands out a midterm worth 40% of the grade. Students study hard, take the test, and receive scores a week later. Many did poorly, but by then, the class had moved on. The exam was an ending, not a tool for growth.
- **Teacher B** uses frequent, low-stakes checks throughout the term: quick quizzes, reflective questions, and group problem-solving. Students always know where they stand. When the midterm arrives, it isn't a surprise; it's confirmation of progress already tracked.

Both teachers covered the same content. Only one used feedback to fuel growth.

Trainer and Professor Insights

This isn't just about K–12. Professors and workplace trainers face the same choice.

- A professor who waits until the final exam to reveal gaps leaves students stranded. But one who offers weekly practice problems with annotated feedback equips students to adjust long before grades are final.
- A corporate trainer who ends with a pass/fail test may check compliance but won't improve skill. A trainer who pauses

mid-session to say, *"Good start on that sales pitch—now try opening with a question instead of a fact,"* builds competence in real time.

Feedback is universal. It's just as vital in boardrooms and workshops as in classrooms.

When Feedback Changes Everything

I once had a student, let's call him Daniel, who consistently turned in essays filled with strong ideas but weak structure. Early in my career, I might have written "C, work on organization" at the top and moved on.

But when I began practicing constant checks, I responded differently. After each draft, I gave Daniel concrete, actionable steps:

- "Start with your strongest point."
- "Break up long paragraphs."
- "Add transitions to guide the reader."

By the end of the semester, Daniel's essays had transformed. More importantly, so had his confidence. The growth didn't come from the grade; it came from feedback and the realization that his work was improving.

The Employer's View

Employers often complain that new hires lack resilience. But beneath that is something deeper: Many graduates interpret feedback as failure. Why? Because in school, they were conditioned to see the grade as the final word.

In reality, workplace success depends on constant guidance. Nearly 90% of employers say they are looking for problem-solving ability in new hires, with teamwork, communication, and adaptability close behind (NACE, 2024). Yet surveys reveal a 25% or greater gap between how proficient graduates believe they are and how employers rate them (NACE, 2024). This gap doesn't exist because students don't care; it exists because feedback in education failed to prepare them for feedback in life.

High-performing workplaces don't use feedback as punishment; they use it as progress. Employees who grew up in classrooms with constant checks carry a different mindset. They expect guidance, welcome mentoring, and adapt quickly. These are the employees who thrive.

Why Grades Fail and Feedback Transforms

Grades freeze learning in place; feedback moves it forward. It doesn't just measure the past; it transforms the learner, turning mistakes into mastery and equipping them with the confidence, resilience, and adaptability the real world demands.

Feedback transforms because it:

- Makes learning continuous instead of episodic.
- Encourages a growth mindset instead of a fixed one.
- Builds resilience by normalizing mistakes as steppingstones, not dead ends.

In short… grades close the book, feedback opens it.

Grades vs. Feedback: The Real Difference

Grades Say…	Feedback Adds…	Example Comments (Varied Contexts)
A → "You did well."	Explains why it was strong.	"Your lab report clearly linked the hypothesis to the results… excellent reasoning." (Science)
C → "You're struggling."	Shows what needs fixing and how to fix it.	"Your math solution is correct, but you skipped key steps. Write them out so others can follow." (Math)
F → "You failed."	Offers a pathway forward.	"This coding project didn't run because of missing syntax. Let's debug one line together so you can apply it to the rest." (Technology)
85% → "You're average."	Targets improvement in a specific skill.	"Your essay has strong analysis, but the conclusion ends abruptly. Add a final sentence tying back to your thesis." (Writing)
Pass/Fail	Misses the chance for growth.	"Good effort on the group project. Next time, contribute earlier so your ideas shape the outcome." (Collaboration)

Key Takeaway

- **Grades = Judgment** (past-focused, static)
- **Feedback = Guidance** (future-focused, actionable, specific across disciplines)

Feedback isn't just for essays. It applies to labs, machines, presentations, sports, and teamwork. Wherever there's performance, there's room for feedback.

Directed feedback is the GPS of learning: It doesn't just tell you where you are; it tells you how to adjust your route to reach the destination.

The Bigger Picture

Our society craves instant gratification, but we must resist turning education into little more than a scoreboard of grades. Yes, grades can open or close doors, but meaningful feedback is what helps students walk through those doors confidently. When feedback is given, students can choose whether to accept it or not, but as educators, trainers, and professors, we cannot deny them the opportunity.

Students don't need more grades. They need more guidance. They need more constant checks. They need teachers and trainers willing to pause, point out the progress, and push them toward the next step.

Looking Ahead

So far, we've examined curiosity, clarity, connection, examples, and now feedback. But even the best feedback fades without one final ingredient: practice. That's where we're headed next, Chapter Seven: *Learning That Lasts*, where we'll see why application is the difference between information forgotten and transformation lived.

Chapter Seven

Learning That Lasts

The Statistic That Should Concern Us All

Studies on memory retention have revealed a sobering truth: Students forget up to 90% of what they learn within thirty days if they don't apply it (Bahrick, 1984). Thirty days after finals week, most of the late nights, frantic note-taking, and highlighted passages have faded into nothing.

This isn't because students are careless; it's because the human brain retains what it uses and lets go of what it doesn't. Without application, learning simply doesn't last (Cepeda et al., 2006; Roediger & Butler, 2011).

Recent research confirms this. Strategies like retrieval practice and spaced repetition significantly strengthen retention and promote transfer into new contexts (Kranz, 2024; Yao et al., 2025). In medical training, spaced repetition has improved exam scores by more than 20% (Burel et al., 2025). When paired with active learning, retention rates climb even higher and failure rates plummet (Freeman et al., 2014; Driessen et al., 2023).

The truth is simple: What we apply, we keep. What we don't apply, we lose.

The Deception: Memorization Equals Mastery

Education often rewards those who can memorize and repeat information. Cramming the night before the exam, pouring out facts on the test, and forgetting them days later... this cycle has been normalized as "success."

But memorization is not mastery. It is short-term recall. Real mastery comes from using knowledge through testing, practicing, struggling, and reflecting.

I saw this countless times with my own students.

A Student's Story

One of my students, Sarah, was a master at cramming. She could memorize a thick stack of notes in a night and score high on exams. But weeks later, she admitted: "I don't remember any of it. I studied for the test, not for myself."

Sarah wasn't failing the system; in fact, the system was failing her. She was rewarded for memorization when what she needed was practice.

When I began requiring application projects, where students had to use what they learned in real scenarios, and Sarah's performance changed. She not only remembered concepts, but she also began to see herself as capable, creative, and resourceful.

Research backs this. Students in active learning environments retain significantly more than their lecture-only peers, perform better on assessments, and gain confidence in their ability to apply knowledge in new situations (Gilbert, 2023; Freeman et al., 2014).

Why Application Matters

Without application:

- Students may pass exams but lack confidence.
- Employers must reteach skills that should have been mastered in school.
- Society loses out on innovators who can think critically and adapt quickly.

With application:

- Memory strengthens through practice (Cepeda et al., 2006).
- Theory becomes a transferable skill (Kolb, 1984).
- Resilience grows through trial and error (Ericsson et al., 1993).

Application is where information becomes transformation.

TEA4CH™ Spotlight: Application

Information is forgotten; application is remembered. What we practice, we keep.

Application: From Knowing to Doing

Application is the step that turns education into empowerment. It's where students practice actively, reflect deeply, and build skills that stick.

Why Application Matters ~ With Data

- Spaced repetition improves both short- and long-term retention (Burel et al., 2025; Durrani, 2024).
- Active learning reduces failure rates by more than half (Freeman et al., 2014; Driessen et al., 2023).
- Retrieval practice strengthens durable memory and transfer (Roediger & Butler, 2011; Kranz, 2024).
- AI-generated practice has boosted student test performance by 16 percentage points (An et al., 2025).

What Application Looks Like in TEA4CH™

- **Hands-on projects** that require using concepts in real-world ways.
- **Reflection journals** where students process what worked and what didn't.
- **Role plays and simulations** that mimic the workplace.
- **Action steps** that encourage students to take their learning beyond the classroom.

Application isn't extra; in fact, it's essential. Without it, knowledge evaporates. With it, knowledge multiplies.

A Tale of Two Teachers

- **Professor: Lecture-Only:** ends a unit with a high-stakes exam. Students memorize, perform, and promptly forget. The test becomes a finish line, not a stepping-stone.
- **Professor: Applied-Learning:** teaches the same material but ends with a project. Students must design a solution, test

their ideas, and present outcomes. The exam isn't the end but the evidence of what they can do.

Both cover content. Only one ensures the learning lasts.

The Apprenticeship Advantage

Think about why apprenticeships and internships work so well.

A welding student can study techniques for months, but the first time they hold the torch, the learning becomes real. A nursing student can memorize anatomy charts endlessly, but the first time they insert an IV, the lesson becomes unforgettable.

Application is why apprenticeships consistently produce confident, capable graduates, while lecture-heavy programs produce uncertain ones. It isn't just about doing the work, it's about *learning through doing*.

This reflects what Ericsson et al. (1993) called *deliberate practice*... structured, repeated application that builds expertise.

The Employer's Perspective

Employers often describe graduates as "book smart but not job-ready." The National Association of Colleges and Employers (2024) found that while 89% of employers want problem-solving ability, fewer than half of graduates demonstrate it.

A business leader once told me: "I don't need employees who can recite a textbook. I need employees who can solve problems when the answer isn't in the book."

Application trains that muscle. It teaches students to face ambiguity, to improvise, and to take what they've learned and shape it into solutions.

Learning That Lasts: The Skills Students Need

Without Application	With Application
Memorization fades within weeks.	Memory sticks through practice and use.
Students know *what* to think.	Students learn *how* to think.
Exams feel like finish lines.	Projects feel like steppingstones.
Employers must retrain graduates.	Employers gain job-ready contributors.
Students doubt their abilities.	Students grow in confidence and resilience.

The Lifelong Impact

Application doesn't just prepare students for jobs; it prepares them for life. When students practice applying knowledge, they also practice:

- **Decision-making**: weighing options, anticipating consequences.
- **Communication**: articulating ideas clearly.

- **Adaptability**: shifting when circumstances change.
- **Confidence**: knowing they can learn from failure.

These are not only workplace skills, they're life skills (Kolb, 1984; Roediger & Butler, 2011).

A Classroom Transformation

When I redesigned one of my courses to emphasize application, everything changed. Instead of ending each unit with a test, I asked students to apply the concepts to real-world problems.

One group created a business plan. Another designed a community outreach initiative. Another analyzed workplace case studies.

The results were dramatic: Students were engaged, creative, and proud of their work. They weren't just learning, they were becoming.

The most powerful example came from a student I'll call Jose. His project began as a classroom assignment but grew into a business that provided affordable memorial services for grieving families.

Jose's story was even more remarkable because of where he started. He had recently been released from prison and was in school as part of a mandated program. Yet when given the chance to apply what he was learning, he not only discovered purpose, he also built a future.

That's what application does. It transforms knowledge into confidence, projects into livelihoods, and learners into leaders.

Looking Ahead

We've now walked through the pillars of TEA4CH™: Curiosity, Clarity, Teaching, Connection, Example, Constant Checks, and Application. Each piece matters on its own. Together, they form a framework that can move education from deception to transformation.

That's what we'll explore in Chapter Eight: *From Deception to Transformation*, how all the pieces come together to create an education that doesn't just hand out diplomas but equips students for life.

PART II
THE TRANSFORMATION

Chapter Eight

From Deception to Transformation

The Truth We Can't Ignore

Every year, over four million students graduate from U.S. colleges and universities. They cross stages, turn tassels, and clutch diplomas that symbolize years of effort and investment. Yet a troubling number graduate without the critical thinking, communication, and problem-solving skills they need to thrive.

One landmark study revealed that 45% of college students show no significant improvement in critical thinking, reasoning, or writing after two years of study, and 36% show no improvement after four years (Arum & Roksa, 2021). Employers echo this concern; nearly 50% report difficulty finding graduates with adequate problem-solving and communication skills (National Association of Colleges and Employers [NACE], 2022). And in a rapidly changing economy, adaptability is just as critical: 63% of employers rank adaptability and resilience among the most important skills for career success, yet only 35% believe recent graduates are adequately prepared in these areas (World Economic Forum, 2023).

The deception isn't in the diploma itself; it's in believing the diploma guarantees readiness. But deception doesn't have to be destiny. Transformation is possible.

We've Pulled Back the Curtain

Throughout this book, we've peeled back the layers of what I call Diploma Deception:

- The Illusion of Success: Seat time mistaken for skill.
- The Shocking Truth About Teaching: Professors untrained in pedagogy.
- Why Lecture Fails: Passive listening disguised as learning.
- What Students Really Need: Connection between student and teacher.
- Real-World vs. Classroom: Knowledge without context crumbling under pressure.
- The Missing Feedback Loop: Grades substituting for guidance.
- Learning That Lasts: Memorization mistaken for mastery.

Each illusion has a cost, paid by students, employers, and society. But each chapter also revealed a way forward through the TEA4CH™ method.

The Complete TEA4CH™ Framework

When practiced together, the seven pillars of TEA4CH™ move education from deception to transformation:

1. Curiosity – Spark wonder and invite questions.
2. Clarity – Define goals and simplify complexity.
3. Teaching – Model processes and provide strategies.
4. Connection – Make learning personal and relational.

5. Example – Anchor content in real-world stories and case studies.
6. Constant Checks – Give timely feedback that fuels growth.
7. Application – Ensure knowledge is practiced and lived.

This isn't theory; it's a roadmap. Each element addresses a gap, and together they form a method that changes not only how students learn but how they live. Research confirms that active learning strategies, especially those integrating curiosity, feedback, and application, result in significantly higher student outcomes than lecture-based models (Freeman et al., 2021; Prince & Felder, 2022).

TEA4CH™ Spotlight

When education shifts from passive information transfer to active transformation, diplomas stop being symbols of deception and become proof of preparation.

The TEA4CH™ model benefits:

- **Teachers, Professors, and Trainers** – Gain tools that engage rather than exhaust, and see measurable growth in learners.
- **Parents and Homeschool Educators** – Move beyond rote memory toward relational learning.
- **Students** – Leave classrooms not just with knowledge but with confidence, adaptability, and skill.
- **Employers** – Gain workers who think critically, communicate effectively, and apply knowledge in real-world contexts.

Traditional Lecture vs. TEA4CH™

Aspect	Traditional Lecture	TEA4CH™ Method
Role of Student	Passive listener	Active participant and co-creator
Role of Teacher	Information deliverer	Guide, mentor, facilitator
Engagement	Minimal; attention often wanes after 10 min	Sustained; curiosity and interaction drive it
Learning Approach	Memorization-focused	Critical thinking, problem-solving, application
Feedback	Grades at end of unit or test	Constant checks, real-time adjustments
Connection	Rare; one-way communication	Strong; personal, relational
Career Readiness	Weak; graduates often lack transferable skills	Strong; students practice communication, adaptability, collaboration

The Ripple Effect

When educators embrace TEA4CH™, the impact ripples outward:

- Students leave not just informed but empowered, confident, adaptable, and ready for whatever comes next.
- Employers gain graduates who can think critically, collaborate, and solve problems.
- Communities benefit from citizens who know how to listen, engage, and contribute.
- Families see children grow into capable adults, not just credentialed ones.

The transformation goes beyond the workplace. It equips people with life skills: communication, resilience, empathy, and adaptability. Skills that matter in marriages, in parenting, in leadership, and in civic life (OECD, 2023).

A Story of Transformation

One professor who adopted TEA4CH™ shared this with me: "I used to lecture and wonder why students weren't engaged. Now I start with curiosity, connect to their experiences, and build in constant checks. My students not only understand more but also believe more in themselves. Their confidence has soared."

That's transformation. Not because the content changed but because the approach changed.

From Information to Transformation

The truth is—information has never been more accessible. Students can Google facts, stream lectures, and watch tutorials. What they can't Google is the transformation that happens when a teacher guides them through curiosity, clarity, connection, and application.

That's the difference between education as information delivery and education as life preparation (Deslauriers, McCabe, & Persellin, 2019; Hora, 2021).

A Call to Action

This book isn't just for professors, teachers, or trainers. It's for anyone who believes education should be more than a diploma.

- Educators: Adopt one element of TEA4CH™ in your next class. Notice the change.
- Students: Demand more than lectures and grades. Seek connection, feedback, and application.
- Employers: Partner with educators to close the skills gap. Ask not just what graduates know but what they can do.
- Parents: Advocate for schools that teach for life, not just for tests.

Together, we can move from deception to transformation.

Looking Ahead

We began this chapter with a sobering reality: Nearly half of students show little to no measurable progress in critical thinking after years in higher education. We close with a vision: classrooms, campuses, and communities alive with engagement, feedback, and application.

Diplomas will still matter. But what they represent will matter more. They will no longer be deceptive tokens of seat time but true reflections of skills, competence, and transformation. That is the future TEA4CH™ makes possible.

And yet this is only the beginning. The framework is powerful, but what happens if we fail to act on it? What are the costs to students, parents, employers, and communities if the current system continues unchanged? Those questions lead us directly into the next chapter: *The Cost of Doing Nothing*. Because understanding the method is not enough, we must also recognize the consequences of ignoring it.

Chapter Nine

The Cost of Doing Nothing

The Price of Silence

We've seen the promise of transformation through the TEA4CH™ framework. But what happens if nothing changes? What if schools, colleges, and training programs continue on the same path, handing out diplomas without delivering real preparation?

The cost of doing nothing is staggering. It's not just borne by students but ripples outward into families, employers, communities, and the economy itself.

- For students, it means graduating with debt but without direction, carrying credentials but lacking confidence.
- For parents, it means investing in tuition only to see their children return home, unemployed or underemployed.
- For employers, it means spending billions on retraining workers who should have been prepared before stepping onto the job.
- For society, it means innovation stalls, leadership falters, and the workforce struggles to adapt in a rapidly changing world.

A recent report found that U.S. employers spend more than $180 billion annually on employee training and development, much of it aimed at teaching basic communication, problem-solving, and adaptability skills that should have been mastered long before the first day on the job (Association for Talent Development [ATD], 2022). This isn't just inefficiency, it's waste. Waste of money, time, potential, and trust.

And if we're honest, we've watched this erosion for decades. Since the early 2000s, and especially after the COVID-19 pandemic, the cracks widened into chasms. Students fell behind, teacher shortages grew, and "learning loss" became a household phrase. The decline isn't subtle anymore; it's visible in test scores, in classrooms, and in the workplace. Doing nothing is no longer an option; the cost is already too high.

The Student's Cost: Debt Without Direction

Consider Maya, a first-generation college student who followed every step she was told would lead to success: attend classes, complete assignments, graduate. She earned her degree in business administration, but when she landed her first job, her manager quickly realized she lacked the ability to analyze problems independently or communicate solutions clearly. Maya's diploma opened the door, but her skills couldn't keep her inside.

She's not alone. Nearly 41% of recent graduates are underemployed, working in jobs that don't require their degree, and many remain stuck in that cycle for years (Burning Glass Institute, 2022). For these students, the cost is both financial and emotional: loan payments without meaningful income, and dreams deferred by a system that promised preparation but delivered only paper.

I've taught too many "Mayas" in my classrooms. Bright, capable, eager but cheated by a system that measured attendance and test scores rather than skills and readiness. When they hit the workforce, the realization is crushing. The diploma may open a door, but without the ability to think critically and adapt, it doesn't hold the key to staying in the room.

The Parents' Cost: Investment Without Return

Parents, too, pay the price. They save for years, often sacrificing their own financial security, believing their investment will give their children a future. Yet many parents now see their children moving back home after graduation, burdened with debt and underemployment.

The average family contribution to higher education has reached $26,373 per student per year when combining savings, income, and borrowing (College Board, 2023). When students emerge unprepared, parents feel not only the financial weight but the heartbreak of broken trust.

I've seen firsthand the sacrifices families make for education. And when the system fails to deliver? The wound isn't just financial, it's deeply personal. Parents send their children to college full of hope, only to see that hope unravel into disappointment.

The Employer's Cost: Billions in Retraining

Employers bear perhaps the most visible cost. A manufacturing CEO once told me, *"We don't mind training workers on our processes. But why are we spending months teaching college graduates how to think, solve problems, or write a professional email?"*

This frustration is reflected in data: 44% of employers say they cannot find candidates with the soft skills they need, particularly adaptability, teamwork, and problem-solving (NACE, 2022). The World Economic Forum (2023) further reports that adaptability and resilience top the list of future skills, but only a third of graduates demonstrate readiness.

For employers, this means massive retraining costs, lost productivity, and high turnover. For the economy, it means an untapped workforce and slower innovation. Every hour spent reteaching skills that should have been mastered in school is an hour not spent on growth, creativity, or advancement.

The Societal Cost: A Weakening Foundation

When students graduate unprepared, when parents lose faith in education, and when employers struggle to find capable workers, the entire fabric of society frays. Communities lose out on leadership, creativity, and civic engagement. Democracies weaken when citizens lack critical thinking and the ability to separate fact from fiction.

The Organisation for Economic Co-operation and Development (OECD, 2023) warns that societies unable to cultivate lifelong learning risk widening inequality, declining productivity, and social fragmentation. Doing nothing is not neutral; it actively harms the next generation and the stability of the world they will come to inherit.

And we're already seeing it. In the past decade, test scores in reading and math have stagnated or declined in many states, and post-pandemic reports highlight the largest learning losses in a generation (Kuhfeld et al., 2022). If we don't act, today's "learning loss" will become tomorrow's "leadership loss."

Why TEA4CH™ Matters Now

Here lies the turning point. Until now, no cohesive, research-driven, classroom-tested framework existed that addressed all of these gaps at once. Educators might try active learning in pieces, or trainers might experiment with case studies, but there was no holistic, practical model that brought together curiosity, clarity, connection, example, feedback, and application.

The TEA4CH™ Method is that catalyst. It equips educators with tools to transform passive learning into active growth. It empowers students to leave classrooms not only informed but prepared. It relieves parents by ensuring their investment builds real capability. And it restores confidence for employers that a diploma means more than attendance… it means readiness.

Doing nothing keeps us locked in the cycle of waste and disappointment. Doing something, adopting TEA4CH™, breaks the cycle and reclaims education as a pathway to life readiness.

Looking Ahead

The cost of doing nothing is too high for students, too heavy for parents, too expensive for employers, and too dangerous for society.

We cannot sit silently as education drifts further from its purpose. We must rise up, demand better, and act boldly for the sake of students, for the strength of our communities, and for the future of our world.

The choice is clear: continue paying for failure or invest in transformation.

In the next chapter, we will look at an often-overlooked partner in this transformation: parents. Their role in education doesn't end when they write tuition checks. In fact, their involvement may be the missing key in bridging schools and real-world readiness.

Chapter Ten

Parents as Partners

The First Teachers

Long before children enter a classroom, they are already learning. Parents are their first teachers, guiding language, modeling behavior, and demonstrating values. Every bedtime story, every moment of encouragement, every example set at home teaches children how to think, relate, and grow.

Consider this: If parents taught their children only by lecturing, never showing, never modeling, never demonstrating, how much would children truly learn? A toddler doesn't master walking because of a lecture; she learns by watching, trying, falling, and being encouraged to try again. A child doesn't learn honesty through a definition in a book; he learns when he sees his parents tell the truth, even when it costs something.

In other words, parents instinctively use TEA4CH™ principles long before they know the name: They spark curiosity by answering endless "why" questions, they provide clarity through routines, they teach by modeling behaviors, they connect with love and attention, they give examples in daily life, they offer constant checks through correction and guidance, and they ensure application as children put lessons into practice.

This is why parents play a vital role in education reform. They already embody TEA4CH at home. When they entrust schools, colleges, and universities with their children, they expect that same model of engagement, not a cold replacement with endless lectures.

The Parent-School Disconnect

Yet research shows that the connection between parents and schools often weakens as children get older. In early childhood, parental involvement is celebrated. But by middle school and especially in high school and college, parents are expected to "step back."

The result is a troubling disconnect. A national survey found that over 70% of parents of high school and college students feel shut out of their child's educational experience, even while contributing tens of thousands of dollars toward tuition (Learning Heroes, 2022). Meanwhile, only 27% of parents strongly agree that schools are preparing students with the life skills they need (Gallup & Walton Family Foundation, 2021).

This disconnect doesn't only affect academics; it carries over into the workplace. Parents know from their own careers that success requires more than memorized facts. It requires problem-solving, adaptability, collaboration, and communication. When schools fail to cultivate these skills, parents see the gap immediately because they live it daily in their own professional worlds.

Parents as Catalysts for Career Readiness

Parents aren't just investors in their children's education; they're participants in the workforce. They know what it takes to succeed in a job, advance in a career, and contribute to a team. They understand deadlines, leadership, accountability, and adaptability because they practice them at work every day.

This lived experience makes parents uniquely qualified to demand that schools prepare students not just to pass tests but to thrive in professional environments. Employers echo this demand: Surveys consistently show that communication, teamwork, and critical thinking outrank technical expertise as the most desired skills for new hires (National Association of Colleges and Employers [NACE], 2023).

The good news is that communities across the country are creating programs to close this gap. For example, the **CareerLaunch program** from the Boys & Girls Clubs of America provides structured opportunities for teens to explore careers, develop employability skills, and connect with mentors who help bridge school and work (Boys & Girls Clubs of America, n.d.). Similarly, the **Urban Youth Pathways program** from the National Urban League offers career coaching, job placement support, and internships for under-represented youth, ensuring that career readiness begins well before college graduation (National Urban League, n.d.).

In New York City, the Department of Youth & Community Development operates the **Career Readiness and Modern Youth Apprenticeship initiative**, which pairs high school students with paid internships and professional mentors, giving them exposure to "day in the life" experiences across industries (New York City Department of Youth & Community Development, n.d.). In Chicago, **Youth Guidance's Career Readiness and Success programs** combine social-emotional learning with workforce training, recognizing that emotional intelligence and resilience are just as critical as technical know-how (Youth Guidance, n.d.).

Even at the local community level, programs like **Youth Express from Keystone Community Services in St. Paul, Minnesota** provide hands-on workforce development and leadership training for middle and high school students, ensuring that career readiness is not left until the college years but begins early in adolescence (Keystone Community Services, n.d.).

These programs echo the very principles of TEA4CH™: clarity through goal setting, connection through mentorship, curiosity through exploration, and application through hands-on practice. Parents, as the first teachers, can advocate for and connect their children to opportunities like these while also modeling skills at home and encouraging exploration in their communities.

Helping Children Explore Options Early

One important feature parents can add is helping their children explore what might be possible long before high school graduation. High school, and even middle school, should be a time for exploration, not just of classes but of paths, of possibilities, of what life might look like after school.

- **Expose early:** Take children (as young as 7 or 8) to career fairs, "a day in the life" experiences, or volunteer days. Let them spend a day or half-day shadowing someone in a trade, health, arts, business, agriculture, etc.

- **Encourage volunteer work and community involvement**: Volunteering teaches responsibility, communication, teamwork, and gives a window into many professions.
- **Internships and apprenticeships**: In high school, encourage your child to take internships or even job shadowing. Schools and communities increasingly offer programs that allow students to try things out.
- **Part-time job & entrepreneurship**: Getting a first paying job (or small business experience) builds work habits, time management, interpersonal skills, and accountability.
- **Career assessments & counseling**: Many school districts provide career counseling, aptitude tests, and personality inventories (e.g., interest inventories) that help a student see what careers align with their strengths and passions.
- **Soft skills at home**: Practice communication, resilience, and problem-solving in everyday situations. Let children help plan family tasks, budget allowances, debate ideas, and lead small projects so they learn to think, decide, and reflect.

These programs show two things:

1. It is possible for schools, communities, and parents to work together to provide real exposure and choice.
2. Skills beyond academics—soft skills, decision-making, adaptability—are being taught when the systems make space for them.

The Ripple Effect of Parental Involvement

Parental engagement is not only symbolic; it has a measurable impact. Students with engaged parents:

- Earn higher grades and test scores.
- Have better social skills and classroom behavior.
- Are more likely to graduate and pursue higher education (Wang & Sheikh-Khalil, 2014).

Even in higher education, parental support continues to matter. A 2021 study found that college students who reported strong parental encouragement had higher resilience, greater adaptability, and better academic persistence (Cutrona et al., 2021). These are the very skills employers prize.

The bridge between home, school, and workplace is clear: When parents reinforce curiosity, clarity, and application at home, students enter school ready to learn in ways that matter. When schools adopt TEA4CH™, they extend those same principles into structured learning. And when both align, the result is graduates who bring value to employers, families, and communities.

TEA4CH™ Spotlight: Parents as Partners in Workforce Readiness

Parents are living proof that lecture alone doesn't work. Children learn by watching, imitating, practicing, and applying. The same is true for preparing for a career. Readiness is not taught in theory alone; it is modeled, tested, and applied in practice.

How Parents Embody TEA4CH™ in Career Readiness:

- **Teaching (Clarity):** Parents can explain workplace expectations, deadlines, accountability, and teamwork in ways that connect to daily life.
- **Example (Connection):** Children watch how parents handle conflict, adapt to change, or manage money. These examples speak louder than lectures.
- **Application:** Encourage children to explore career paths early through job shadowing, volunteering, or programs like *CareerLaunch* (Boys & Girls Clubs of America, n.d.) and *Youth Express* (Keystone Community Services, n.d.).
- **Constant Checks:** Guide them with real-time feedback on responsibility, whether it's managing chores, balancing schoolwork, or sticking with commitments.

A Story That Proves the Point

When I served as director of a youth college program, we exposed children as young as seven to "a day in the life" of various careers. A veterinarian showed them how to care for animals, a police officer walked them through real community responsibilities, and a chef let them experiment in the kitchen. For many of those children, it was the first time they saw themselves in a career beyond the classroom. Parents later told me how those experiences ignited conversations at home about goals, skills, and dreams.

That program confirmed what I already knew: Career readiness doesn't begin at seventeen when college applications are due. It begins much earlier, when children are given the chance to see, touch, and experience the world of work. Parents who provide or advocate for those opportunities give their children not only clarity but also courage to explore and confidence to prepare.

The Result:

When schools, parents, and community programs align, students practice readiness long before their first job. They don't just imagine a career, they rehearse it. By the time they enter the workforce, adaptability, collaboration, and problem-solving aren't abstract skills; they are habits.

A Call to Parents

Parents, you are not passive observers in education; you are powerful partners.

- Ask schools and universities not just what content they teach but how they prepare students for the realities of work and life.
- Support teachers who use interactive, applied methods by reinforcing them at home. Ask your children not just what they learned but how they practiced it.
- Demand accountability from institutions that take your money and your trust but fail to deliver graduates ready for both life and career.
- Model lifelong learning for your children. Show them that education doesn't end with a diploma but continues in every job, every challenge, and every opportunity to grow.

When parents and educators walk together, the TEA4CH™ model doesn't stop at the classroom door. It becomes a way of living that equips the next generation for leadership, relationships, and careers.

Looking Ahead

If parents are the first teachers, then schools and universities should be the continuation of that partnership, not the betrayal of it. Parents understand the workforce, and they know that career readiness is built on broad preparation, not narrow indoctrination. When institutions ignore what parents know instinctively, they not only undermine student success, they undermine trust in education itself.

The next frontier of this transformation lies in technology. In the coming chapter, we will examine *The Digital Classroom Dilemma*, how online tools can either deepen deception or accelerate transformation, depending on how they are used.

Parents know the stakes, educators feel the pressure, and students live the results. TEA4CH™ provides the bridge, but it is a bridge we must choose to cross together.

Chapter Eleven

The Digital Classroom Dilemma

A Double-Edged Sword

Technology has transformed education more in the past two decades than in the previous two centuries. Online learning platforms, digital textbooks, and virtual classrooms promised to democratize knowledge and make learning accessible to anyone, anywhere.

And yet the results have been mixed. For some, digital tools have opened doors to opportunity. For others, they have widened gaps, reduced engagement, and magnified the very problems already embedded in traditional lecture models.

The digital classroom is a double-edged sword: it can either deepen deception or empower transformation.

When Technology Deceives

The rise of digital tools has not automatically meant better learning. In fact, many schools have simply moved the lecture online, replacing chalkboards with slides, and classrooms with video calls. The problem remains the same: passive consumption of information disguised as learning.

During the COVID-19 pandemic, students experienced this firsthand. One global survey found that over 50% of students reported lower motivation and engagement in remote classes, with many citing lack of interaction and feedback as the key reason (UNESCO, 2021).

In other words, technology revealed what lecture had been hiding all along: Information delivery alone is not enough. Without curiosity, connection, and application, screens only magnify disengagement.

When Technology Transforms

But the digital classroom can also be a powerful accelerator, if guided by the right framework. Research shows that when technology is used for active learning, simulation, feedback, and collaboration, student outcomes improve significantly.

- A 2022 meta-analysis found that digital platforms that emphasize interactive learning improved student achievement by nearly 20% compared to lecture-based online instruction (Bond et al., 2022).
- Virtual simulations in fields like healthcare and engineering increased confidence and critical thinking by allowing students to "learn by doing" in safe environments (Cant & Cooper, 2020).
- Adaptive learning systems that provide real-time constant checks help students stay on track and identify gaps in understanding (Pane et al., 2019).

The difference lies not in the tool itself but in the method of use. When digital tools are aligned with TEA4CH™; curiosity, clarity, connection, example, constant checks, and application, they become bridges to deeper engagement rather than barriers.

The TEA4CH™ Digital Lens

So, how does TEA4CH™ change the digital classroom?

- **Curiosity**: Digital platforms can spark curiosity with interactive polls, gamified quizzes, or virtual explorations that invite questions instead of suppressing them.
- **Clarity**: Online dashboards can show goals, progress, and expectations in ways that reduce confusion.
- **Teaching**: Video demonstrations, screen sharing, and digital modeling let instructors show, not just tell, processes.
- **Connection**: Breakout rooms, discussion boards, and messaging apps allow students to connect with peers and teachers, even at a distance.
- **Example**: Case studies, multimedia storytelling, and real-world scenarios bring concepts to life online.
- **Constant Checks**: Online quizzes, instant feedback tools, and adaptive pathways help learners stay engaged and supported.
- **Application**: Simulations, projects, and collaborative digital assignments give students the chance to practice what they've learned.

Technology doesn't replace TEA4CH™, it extends it.

The Workplace Parallel

Parents and employers understand this truth because they live it. In the workplace, technology is everywhere, but its effectiveness depends on how it's used. A team meeting on Zoom can either be a waste of time filled with passive updates or it can be an engaging session with active brainstorming, shared demonstrations, and collaborative problem-solving.

The same principle applies in education. The workplace demands adaptability, digital literacy, and collaborative skills (World Economic Forum, 2023). If schools use technology only to digitize old lectures, students enter the workforce unprepared. But if schools use technology to build adaptability, critical thinking, and collaboration, they send out graduates ready to thrive in any environment.

TEA4CH™ Spotlight: Digital Done Right

The question is not whether technology belongs in education, it's whether we will use it to copy the old model or to create a new one.

Digital classrooms guided by TEA4CH™:

- **Spark curiosity through interactive tools.**
  Example: A science teacher launches a digital poll asking, *"What would happen if gravity suddenly doubled?"*, while a literature professor uses an online annotation tool to let students ask "why" questions in the margins of a shared text.

- **Strengthen clarity with transparent goals.**
  Example: A math instructor posts weekly learning dashboards showing which skills are mastered and which need practice; a corporate trainer uses project-management apps to show step-by-step milestones for onboarding.
- **Reinforce teaching with demonstration and modeling.**
  Example: In nursing, a digital simulation walks students through inserting an IV line; in business courses, instructors record screen-share videos showing how to build financial models in Excel.
- **Build connections even across distance.**
  Example: In a high school history class, breakout rooms allow small groups to debate primary sources; in a leadership seminar, learners use collaborative whiteboards to brainstorm solutions together in real time.
- **Provide examples that feel real and relevant.**
  Example: Engineering students use 3D modeling software to test bridge designs; education majors analyze video case studies of real classrooms to see strategies in action.
- **Deliver constant checks with instant feedback.**
  Example: Language students practice pronunciation with AI speech tools that flag errors instantly; law students use adaptive quiz platforms that adjust based on their answers to sharpen case analysis.
- **Ensure application through simulations and projects.**
  Example: Medical students practice diagnosing virtual patients in a safe online environment; culinary students record and submit cooking demonstrations with peer and instructor feedback.

Without TEA4CH™, technology risks becoming just a shinier version of the lecture. With TEA4CH™, it becomes a lever for transformation.

Digital Lecture vs. Digital TEA4CH™

TEA4CH™ Principle	Lecture-Style Digital Classroom	TEA4CH™ Digital Transformation (with Examples)
Curiosity	Teacher posts a pre-recorded lecture video with no interaction.	Interactive polls in science (*"What if gravity doubled?"*), or collaborative annotation in literature where students pose questions in the margins.
Clarity	Students receive a syllabus PDF at the start of term, rarely revisited.	Weekly dashboards show progress on math skills; onboarding milestones tracked in project-management apps for training.
Teaching (Modeling)	Instructors explain concepts verbally with slides.	Nursing students practice IV insertion through simulation; business instructors record screen shares demonstrating financial models.

TEA4CH™ Principle	Lecture-Style Digital Classroom	TEA4CH™ Digital Transformation (with Examples)
Connection	Students sit muted in video calls; limited chat use.	Breakout rooms for history debates; collaborative whiteboards for leadership brainstorming across distance.
Example	Generic examples given in lectures with little context.	Engineering students test digital bridge designs in 3D modeling; education majors analyze real classroom video cases.
Constant Checks	Grades given at midterms or finals only.	Language learners use AI speech tools for instant pronunciation feedback; law students use adaptive quiz platforms to sharpen case analysis.
Application	Students complete multiple-choice online exams.	Medical students diagnose virtual patients; culinary students upload cooking demos with peer/instructor review.

A Call to Action

Technology isn't neutral. It can perpetuate deception or ignite transformation. The difference depends on whether we use it merely to transmit information or to cultivate the skills that last a lifetime.

Every stakeholder has a role to play. Educators, parents, employers, and even students must press pause and ask:

- **Does this tool encourage curiosity or shut it down?**
  If students can only click "next" on slides, curiosity dies. But when tools invite exploration, like virtual labs where students can test "what if" scenarios, curiosity thrives. In fact, interactive learning tools increase motivation and engagement by over 50% compared to static digital materials (Bond et al., 2022).
- **Does it build connection or isolate learners behind screens?**
  A student alone with headphones may finish a module but feel unseen. Connection grows when technology enables peer collaboration, mentorship, and meaningful dialogue across distance. Research shows that students in digitally connected classrooms report twice the sense of belonging compared to those in lecture-only online environments (OECD, 2023).
- **Does it give feedback that leads to growth or leave students guessing?**
  Waiting weeks for a grade leaves learners in the dark. Instant feedback through adaptive quizzes, simulations, or peer review helps them course-correct in real time, just like the workplace demands. A meta-analysis revealed that immediate feedback improves learning outcomes by an average of 0.43 standard deviations, the difference between struggling and succeeding (Hattie & Timperley, 2020).

- **Does it allow for practice and application or only memorization and recall?**
  Multiple-choice exams test memory, not mastery. But digital projects, role plays, and simulations allow learners to practice, fail safely, and build the resilience they will need on the job. Studies of simulation-based learning show gains of up to 30% in applied problem-solving skills (Cant & Cooper, 2020).

The answers to these questions determine whether the digital classroom widens the gap or closes it.

And the stakes couldn't be higher. The future of education, the readiness of the workforce, and the trust of families depend on how we answer. With TEA4CH™, technology becomes more than a tool; it becomes a lever for transformation.

Looking Ahead

The digital classroom is not going away. If anything, it will expand through AI, virtual reality, and global connectivity. The question is not whether we will use technology but whether we will use it well.

In the next chapter, we will look at *The Future of Education*: how TEA4CH™ can prepare students, parents, educators, and employers to thrive in a world that is rapidly evolving. The digital classroom is just one piece of the puzzle; the larger challenge is building a system that is not only adaptive but also enduring.

Chapter Twelve

The Future of Education

A New Horizon

Education has always been about more than passing knowledge from one generation to the next. At its best, it equips learners to adapt, create, and thrive in a changing world. Yet the world is now changing faster than our education systems can keep up.

By 2030, more than one billion people will need to reskill due to automation, artificial intelligence, and shifting labor markets (World Economic Forum [WEF], 2020). Employers consistently rank adaptability, critical thinking, and digital literacy among the top skills for the future (NACE, 2023; OECD, 2023). And yet our current systems are still graduating students underprepared for this reality.

This isn't just about the future of education. It's about the future of our children, our workforce, and our society.

And here is the sobering truth: We are already behind. COVID-19 left scars that we are still recovering from. Students lost ground academically, socially, and emotionally. Many never regained the learning momentum they once had. Families and educators scrambled to adapt, but the cracks in our systems became craters. And while we talk about "catching up," the world isn't slowing down to wait.

The question before us is urgent: What future are we building if education doesn't transform now?

The Shifting Landscape

Education doesn't exist in a vacuum. It's shaped and often shaken by the forces that define our world. The next decade will bring disruptions we can't afford to ignore:

- **Technology.** Artificial intelligence, virtual reality, and personalized learning platforms are no longer futuristic, they're here. By 2030, AI alone is expected to transform or eliminate up to 30% of current jobs (McKinsey & Company, 2021). If we keep teaching through static lectures, we will be preparing students for jobs that no longer exist.
- **Globalization.** Work is no longer local; it's global. Remote teams are the norm. Cross-cultural collaboration is an everyday expectation. Memorizing world facts isn't enough. Students must learn empathy, communication, and cultural agility.
- **Workforce Evolution.** Careers are no longer linear. Today's graduates are expected to change jobs twelve times on average over their lifetimes (U.S. Bureau of Labor Statistics, 2022). That requires resilience and the ability to learn, unlearn, and relearn.
- **Societal Expectations.** Parents are demanding accountability. Employers are questioning the value of diplomas. Communities are asking whether schools are producing not just test-takers but citizens who can lead, collaborate, and solve real problems.

The ground beneath education is shifting. The question isn't whether it will change, it's whether we will shape that change with courage and intention or whether we will let it shape us by default.

TEA4CH™: A Framework for the Future

The good news is this: We don't have to reinvent the wheel. TEA4CH™ isn't bound to a tool, a textbook, or a trend. It's a compass rooted in how humans actually learn.

- **Curiosity** will drive innovation when machines take over repetitive tasks.
- **Clarity** will cut through the noise of a world drowning in information and misinformation.
- **Teaching (Modeling)** will matter more than ever in a world where facts can be Googled.
- **Connection** will ground learning in humanity when technology threatens isolation.
- **Example** will bridge theory and practice, showing students how learning matters in real life.
- **Constant Checks** will thrive in a digital age where real-time feedback is possible.
- **Application** will remain the ultimate test. Knowledge only lasts when it is used.

TEA4CH™ isn't just a teaching method. It's a survival kit for education's future.

> ## TEA4CH™ Spotlight: Education That Lasts
>
> *The true measure of education isn't the diploma in hand but the skills, character, and confidence that endure for a lifetime.*

- **Educators:** Create classrooms alive with curiosity and application.
- **Parents:** You are the first teachers. Partner with schools. Reinforce curiosity and connection at home.
- **Students:** Take ownership. Education isn't done to you; it's built by you.
- **Employers:** Partner with schools. Don't just demand skills, help shape them.
- **Institutions:** Stop protecting outdated lecture models. Make internships, projects, and real-world applications central, not optional.
- **Communities:** Recognize that the future workforce is also the future citizenry. Invest in education reform like your stability depends on it… because it does.

Education that lasts isn't measured by tests or diplomas. It's measured by the lifelong ability to think, solve, adapt, and lead.

The Future Workforce

The World Economic Forum (2023) projects that 44% of workers' skills will be disrupted within the next five years. That means today's students are preparing for a workforce we can barely predict. Employers aren't just asking for technical expertise; they're demanding "power skills": adaptability, resilience, empathy, and collaboration (McKinsey & Company, 2021).

And here's the truth: TEA4CH™ builds those very skills. Curiosity fosters innovation. Clarity creates confidence. Connection fosters empathy. Constant Checks normalize resilience. Application cements adaptability.

The future workforce doesn't need more diplomas. It needs more preparation.

The Global Vision

This isn't just an American issue. UNESCO (2022) has called for a "new social contract" for education, one that emphasizes equity, lifelong learning, and collaboration across borders. TEA4CH™ offers a universal framework that works in rural classrooms, homeschool settings, trade schools, universities, and corporate training centers.

The future of education must be global, because the future of the workforce already is.

A Call to Action

We cannot afford to wait. Every year we delay, another generation of students enters the world less prepared than they deserve to be. The cost of doing nothing is too high: financially, socially, and morally.

So, I ask:

- Will we keep handing out diplomas as symbols of attendance or will we demand they represent true preparation?

- Will we keep pouring billions into retraining, or will we finally equip students from the start?
- Will we allow COVID's setbacks to define us, or will we rise up and define a better future?

This is our moment. The future of education isn't just about schools, systems, or policies. It's about people: students, parents, educators, and employers, coming together to demand more and to do more.

Transformation won't happen by accident. It will happen because we chose to act. And the time to act is now.

Closing Vision

Epilogue

Beyond the Diploma

More Than a Milestone

Graduation day is filled with symbolism: caps tossed into the air, tassels turned, and diplomas handed proudly across a stage. For families, it is a moment of celebration. For students, it represents years of effort. And for society, it signals the transition from education to the "real world."

But we now know what the numbers reveal: For too many, a diploma is not a guarantee of readiness. It can be a symbol of perseverance without proof of preparation, a piece of paper without the power to launch a life. The deception isn't in the diploma itself; it's in the belief that the diploma alone is enough.

If this book has revealed anything it's that the cycle of doing the same thing—lecturing, memorizing, testing, graduating—without transformation is not sustainable. We cannot afford to continue teaching students *what* to think. We must equip them with the courage, curiosity, and skills to discover *how* to think, so they can pursue truth long after the classroom lights dim.

Breaking the Cycle

To transform teaching is to break the cycle. To elevate education is to refuse to accept mediocrity when excellence is possible. It's to demand that classrooms become places where students don't parrot answers but wrestle with questions. It's to require that education move beyond indoctrination, telling students what to believe, and toward true formation, teaching them how to seek, test, and discern what is true.

This isn't about stripping away opinions or silencing perspectives. It's about preparing students to sift through complexity, to evaluate evidence, and to think critically for themselves. Truth is not threatened by honest inquiry; it is revealed through it. And it is truth, not rote memorization, that equips the next generation to lead.

We no longer need to be stuck in a system that confuses knowledge with wisdom or information with preparation. The future depends on whether we raise graduates who can think independently, adapt faithfully, and stand firmly in the truth they have discovered.

Beyond the Diploma

The diploma is still an important milestone. It represents achievement, discipline, and perseverance. But it must no longer be the end of the story. What matters most is what students carry beyond the diploma… the skills, habits, and values that equip them to thrive no matter where they go or what they do.

- The adaptability to face challenges that have no clear answers.
- The resilience to keep trying when they fail.
- The curiosity to keep learning long after graduation.
- The integrity to lead with character in the workplace and beyond.

- The empathy to connect across differences and contribute to the community.
- And above all, the capacity to think critically, discern truth, and act wisely.

These are the outcomes that matter. These are the legacies of education that lasts.

The Call for Change

Change will not come easily. For too long, higher education has leaned on lecture and compliance, rewarding students for repeating what they are told rather than for seeking truth. But change is possible, and necessary.

It requires courage to admit that the old ways are not enough. It requires humility to embrace new methods. It requires faithfulness to commit to teaching not what to think but how to think so that truth becomes the guiding principle of every classroom, every training program, and every workplace.

The cycle can be broken. The deception can end. The transformation can begin. But it will not happen by accident. It will happen because we stand together and decide that education is too important to leave unchanged.

Our Shared Responsibility

The future of education isn't the responsibility of teachers alone. It belongs to all of us.

- **Educators** must adopt methods that cultivate curiosity, truth-seeking, and critical thinking.
- **Parents** must reinforce at home that questions are as valuable as answers.
- **Students** must take ownership of their learning, refusing to settle for indoctrination and insisting on transformation.
- **Employers** must support and reward the graduates who bring not just knowledge but wisdom into the workplace.
- **Policymakers** must resist reducing education to test scores and ensure schools are measured by how well they prepare truth-seekers for life.

Final Words

We stand at a crossroads. One path leads to continuing the cycle of diploma deception, of empty milestones, wasted potential, and broken promises. The other path leads to transformation, where education prepares students for work, for relationships, for leadership, for life.

The choice is ours. The need for drastic change is undeniable, but so is the possibility of that change.

If we choose transformation, if we embrace curiosity, clarity, teaching, connection, example, constant checks, and application, then diplomas will no longer be symbols of deception. They will be proof of preparation, confidence, and readiness.

Education will not end at graduation. It will continue for a lifetime. And at the center of it will be students who know not just what to think but how to think… truth-seekers who are prepared for every challenge, every opportunity, and every future.

Beyond the diploma lies the true purpose of education: transformation through truth, learning that lasts, and a legacy that endures.

References

An, Y., Kim, J., & Park, H. (2025). AI-assisted retrieval practice and its impact on student learning outcomes. *Journal of Educational Technology Research, 41*(2), 115–132.

Arum, R., & Roksa, J. (2011). *Academically adrift: Limited learning on college campuses.* University of Chicago Press.

Arum, R., & Roksa, J. (2021). *Limited learning revisited: The long-term impact of college on critical thinking.* Stanford University Press.

Association for Talent Development (ATD). (2022). *2022 State of the Industry Report.* ATD Research.

Bahrick, H. P. (1984). Semantic memory content in permastore: Fifty years of memory for Spanish learned in school. *Journal of Experimental Psychology: General, 113*(1), 1–29.

Black, P., & Wiliam, D. (1998). Assessment and classroom learning. *Assessment in Education: Principles, Policy & Practice, 5*(1), 7–74.

Bligh, D. A. (2000). *What's the use of lectures?* Jossey-Bass.

Bureau of Labor Statistics (BLS). (2022). *Number of jobs, labor market experience, and earnings growth: Results from a national longitudinal survey.* U.S. Department of Labor.

Burel, C., Nguyen, T., & Singh, A. (2025). Spaced repetition in clinical education: Enhancing knowledge retention and application. *Medical Education, 59*(1), 54–67.

Burning Glass Institute. (2022). *The underemployment problem: Recent graduates and the struggle for meaningful work.* Burning Glass Institute.

Cepeda, N. J., Pashler, H., Vul, E., Wixted, J. T., & Rohrer, D. (2006). Distributed practice in verbal recall tasks: A review and quantitative synthesis. *Psychological Bulletin, 132*(3), 354–380.

College Board. (2023). *Trends in college pricing and student aid 2023*. College Board Research.

Cutrona, C. E., Russell, D. W., & Brown, P. A. (2021). Parental support and college student outcomes: The role of resilience and persistence. *Journal of College Student Development, 62*(4), 439–455.

Deslauriers, L., McCarty, L. S., Miller, K., Callaghan, K., & Kestin, G. (2019). Measuring actual learning versus feeling of learning in response to being actively engaged in the classroom. *Proceedings of the National Academy of Sciences, 116*(39), 19251–19257.

Driessen, E., van der Vleuten, C., & Tigelaar, D. (2023). Active learning revisited: Why it works and what still needs to be done. *Medical Teacher, 45*(2), 123–132.

Durrani, H. (2024). Revisiting spaced learning: Applications for modern classrooms. *Journal of Cognitive Education, 32*(1), 45–61.

Ericsson, K. A., Krampe, R. T., & Tesch-Römer, C. (1993). The role of deliberate practice in the acquisition of expert performance. *Psychological Review, 100*(3), 363–406.

Freeman, S., Eddy, S. L., McDonough, M., Smith, M. K., Okoroafor, N., Jordt, H., & Wenderoth, M. P. (2014). Active learning increases student performance in science, engineering, and mathematics. *Proceedings of the National Academy of Sciences, 111*(23), 8410–8415.

Freeman, S., Theobald, R., & Wenderoth, M. P. (2021). Rethinking the lecture: Active learning and student success. *Educational Researcher, 50*(3), 161–169.

Gallup. (2014). *The 2014 Gallup-Lumina Foundation poll on higher education*. Gallup, Inc.

Gallup & Walton Family Foundation. (2021). *Education consumer pulse survey*. Gallup, Inc.

Gilbert, J. (2023). Active learning in higher education: A synthesis of evidence and practice. *Journal of Higher Education Teaching & Learning, 47*(2), 211–229.

Hart Research Associates. (2015). *Falling short? College learning and career success.* Association of American Colleges and Universities.

Hora, M. T. (2021). *Beyond the skills gap: Preparing college students for life and work.* Harvard Education Press.

Kranz, D. (2024). The role of retrieval practice in higher education. *Journal of Applied Cognitive Psychology, 38*(2), 88–102.

Learning Heroes. (2022). *Parents 2022: Going beyond good grades.* Learning Heroes Report.

McKinsey & Company. (2021). *The future of work after COVID-19.* McKinsey Global Institute.

Mueller, P. A., & Oppenheimer, D. M. (2014). The pen is mightier than the keyboard: Advantages of longhand over laptop note taking. *Psychological Science, 25*(6), 1159–1168.

National Association of Colleges and Employers (NACE). (2022). *Job outlook 2022: Attributes employers want to see on college graduates' resumes.*

National Association of Colleges and Employers (NACE). (2023). *Job outlook 2023: Skills employers seek in college graduates.*

Organisation for Economic Co-operation and Development (OECD). (2023). *Education at a glance 2023: OECD indicators.* OECD Publishing.

Prince, M. J., & Felder, R. M. (2022). Inductive teaching and learning revisited. *Journal of Engineering Education, 111*(1), 1–22.

Roediger, H. L., & Butler, A. C. (2011). The critical role of retrieval practice in long-term retention. *Trends in Cognitive Sciences, 15*(1), 20–27.

Theobald, E. J., Hill, M. J., Tran, E., Agrawal, S., Arroyo, E. N., Behling, S., ... Freeman, S. (2020). Active learning narrows achievement gaps for underrepresented students in undergraduate science, technology, engineering, and math. *Proceedings of the National Academy of Sciences, 117*(12), 6476–6483.

UNESCO. (2022). *Reimagining our futures together: A new social contract for education*. UNESCO Publishing.

U.S. Bureau of Labor Statistics. (2022). *Number of jobs, labor market experience, and earnings growth: Results from a national longitudinal survey*. U.S. Department of Labor.

Wang, M.-T., & Sheikh-Khalil, S. (2014). Does parental involvement matter for student achievement and mental health in high school? *Child Development, 85*(2), 610–625.

Wolf, M. (2018). *Reader, come home: The reading brain in a digital world*. Harper.

World Economic Forum. (2020). *The future of jobs report 2020*. WEF.

World Economic Forum. (2023). *Future of jobs report 2023*. WEF.

Yao, X., Lin, Q., & Chen, L. (2025). Spaced learning strategies for long-term knowledge retention. *Learning and Instruction, 85*, 101–115.

Call to Action

Join the Movement Beyond the Diploma

The work of transforming education does not end with this book. Diploma Deception: How the TEA4CH™ Method Transforms Teaching and Elevates Education is only the beginning. The TEA4CH™ framework is not just an idea; it is a blueprint for action, one you can put to work in classrooms, training rooms, corporations, and even at the kitchen table.

TEA4CH™ Consultations

For educators, administrators, or organizations ready for direct support, consultation services are available to help you implement TEA4CH™ most effectively.

- Flexible options: hourly consultations or custom packages depending on your needs.
- Ideal for: classroom teachers, schools, universities, trade schools, corporations, and homeschool groups.
- Focus: actionable strategies, program design, and lasting results.

Your Next Step

Transformation doesn't happen by accident; it happens when people choose to act. Here's how you can begin today:

Join the Movement Beyond the Diploma.

Education can be transformed. TEA4CH™ is how we do it.

www.TEA4CH.com

Final Word

Education will not change because we talk about it.

It will change because we act.

Together, we can end diploma deception and build an education system that prepares every learner not just for graduation but for life.

About the Author

Michelle Van de Sande has devoted more than three decades to education, leadership, and transformation. Known as a teacher's teacher, mentor, and master educator, she has taught at every level of learning, from pre-kindergarten through high school, from community colleges to universities, and into the world of corporate and professional training. She has served as a department chair, curriculum designer, and trainer of trainers, leaving her mark on schools, systems, and organizations across the country.

Michelle's career has been defined by one mission: to make education meaningful. She has served on committees for school improvement and academic change, created innovative curricula adopted by school districts, and designed training programs for national companies that continue to shape how people learn on the job. Her passion has always been to help teachers teach better, students learn deeper, and workplaces build stronger foundations for growth.

Beyond her work in education, Michelle is also a writer and mentor in the areas of faith, relationships, and resilience. She has authored books on marriage and family, on thriving as couples, and on walking with hope through childlessness not by choice. With her husband of thirty-one years, she has guided and mentored engaged and married couples, bringing the same wisdom and empathy to life and relationships that she brings to the classroom.

Her students' work has been published nationally, her teaching recognized with awards including Distinguished Faculty of the Year and Master Teacher designation, and her books honored with an International Book Award. But her greatest satisfaction comes from seeing students, teachers, and readers discover their own capacity to learn, grow, and lead.

In *Diploma Deception: How the TEA4CH™ Method Transforms Teaching and Elevates Education,* Michelle draws on her unmatched vantage point across K–12, higher education, and corporate training to expose the gaps that hold learners back and to offer a bold framework for change. Her passion for education is unmatched, and her legacy is one of transformation.

www.ingramcontent.com/pod-product-compliance
Lightning Source LLC
Chambersburg PA
CBHW072047290426
44110CB00014B/1580